Basic
Income
Imperative

For
Peace, Justice,
Liberty, and
Personal Dignity

Steven Shafarman

Print ISBN: 9781543902044
eBook ISBN: 978-1-5439020-5-1

For true citizens of all lands

Contents

Introduction

The central person in this book is you. Your dreams and goals are core concerns: what you want for yourself, your family, your community, and your country. And what you want from our government and for it as a citizen.

These ideas are more important than their author. My identity and background ought to be irrelevant, and I discuss the reasons in an afterword, From the Author.

Please pretend we're friends. Imagine that you're excited to see me — we haven't been in touch since high school, when we were close, and I'm eager to hear about you. The best way for us to reconnect, I suggest, is for you to read this book. It's short and sincere, and I worked hard to make it pleasant reading.

You might also pretend it was inspired by our shared concerns, and that I wrote it to renew our friendship. It was, in effect, and I did, with questions in every chapter to help us connect. Pause and think about your answers, please.

Even better is thinking aloud. Talk with friends and family, and tell them what you would tell me: What do you like? What would you change? Do you want to work together on the next steps?

I began talking and writing about these ideas in the mid 1980s, and early on I noticed that people's responses reflected their politics, significant differences between liberals and conservatives. Yet I also saw fundamental commonalities. Through listening to many hundreds of people with diverse perspectives, I gleaned vital insights into why our political system is so dysfunctional and – most important – how to renew it.

Those insights inspired and motivated me through the years, and this book is the result. I still have a lot to learn – from you, I hope – yet I now believe this plan is good for everyone: poor and rich, old and young, women and men, rural and urban, healthy and ill and disabled. Specifically, I believe it'll be good for you and your family.

Every day brings more news of real threats to our safety and happiness, and more evidence that our government is broken. Even so, most of us still believe in the American ideals: Free citizens. Life, liberty, and the pursuit of happiness. Equal rights and equal opportunities. Government of the people, by the people, for the people. Liberty and justice for all.

Let's talk about our dreams and goals, and what we can do to achieve them. Let's talk about how to make a better world for our children, our grandchildren, and their great-grandchildren — a better world for everyone. And let's make history.

* * * * *

For readers around the world,

This book is for you, too, though it mainly refers to the United States. You'll find parallels with the political situation where you live, plus prospects for modifying this plan and making it your own. Your country, your plan.

In a democracy, your plan can be a platform for the next election. In a country going through a political transition, you can help ease and speed the passage to a true democracy. In a country with an autocratic ruler or dictator, activists can use these ideas to discreetly attract allies and build support. Your time will come, and you'll be prepared to organize actively, mobilize politically, and succeed quickly.

You and your friends can lead. If your country acts before the United States, I'll thank you. Your efforts could be the catalyst that dissolves the dysfunction in U.S. politics. In our interconnected world, progress anywhere helps people everywhere.

1. We the People

What do I want?

How should I live?

What's best for my family?

These questions lead to thinking about where we live or want to live, the place and the people, our friends and neighbors. Also to thinking about how we earn or want to earn money, and therefore to considering our co-workers, customers, and clients, our employers and perhaps employees. These personal questions connect us to countless people.

Individual citizens are We the People — when we choose to act as such, together. Personal dreams and goals are the keys to progress. The engines are our choices and actions.

As we pursue happiness throughout our lives, we rely on government for our personal safety and national security, and to promote justice and enable commerce. Government issues our money, maintains our police and military, builds roads and other public assets, and enforces laws, rules, and contracts. Government is necessary. Politics, too, because politics is the process we use to select and direct the people who make up our government, and to hold officials accountable.

What do I want? How should I live? That's for me to decide, me and my family; you and your family, other folks and their families. Our decisions ought to be truly ours.

What's best for a neighborhood or community? Who decides? The residents or members, presumably, the folks who have to live with the consequences.

Who decides for your town or city? Your state? Our country? America's Founders gave us an answer: we decide, we individuals acting together as We the People.

> We hold these truths to be self-evident, that all men are created equal, that they are endowed by their creator with certain unalienable rights, that among these are life, liberty, and the pursuit of happiness, — that to secure these rights, governments are instituted among men, deriving their just powers from the consent of the governed, — that whenever any form of government becomes destructive of these ends, it is the right of the people to alter or to abolish it, and to institute new government, laying its foundations on such principles, and organizing its powers in such form, as to them shall seem most likely to effect their safety and happiness.[1]

And:

> We the People of the United States, in order to form a more perfect union, establish justice, insure domestic tranquility, provide for the common defense, promote the general welfare, and secure the blessings of liberty to ourselves and our posterity, do ordain and establish this Constitution.

Individuals with equal rights endowed by our creator, securing our rights by establishing a government. We the People are sovereign and we define our government's roles, duties, powers, and limits. We consent to it and it serves us, each and all of us. Direct relationships with reciprocity between individual citizens and our government.

The Founders' ideals are missing from our everyday experience. Inequality is irrefutable. Reciprocity is only a theory. Consent is passive, most of the time, or partial, fleeting, or conditional. Or consent is coerced.

Our government is broken. It wastes billions of our taxpayers dollars, and is not addressing our concerns. Too many of us are struggling with debts, worrying about our retirement prospects, worrying about our kids and how they'll manage. Most of us are upset or angry about crime, taxes, health care, immigration, global warming, national security, or other issues. But instead of working for us, regular folks, our government mainly serves and supports wealthy special interests.

Our political system is failing, paralyzed by partisan competition. Like rival teams in a major sport, Democrats and Republicans do and say whatever it takes to win. Campaign events are pep rallies. Pundits are coaches, scorekeepers, and cheerleaders.

The two parties are also like rival cliques in a big high school. Each clique is a small band of leaders and insiders, a bunch of wannabes jockeying to become insiders, and a large mass of passive followers. Members use colors, code-words, and cultural references to define and identify themselves, to keep the cliques distinct. The two cliques rule, sharing power or passing it from one to the other. Independent groups and individuals – 40 percent of Americans say they're independent or unaffiliated – are normally excluded, occasionally bribed or bullied.

Our political discourse is polluted, a mess of slogans, sound bites, talking points, platitudes, and euphemisms. *Liberal* is now a synonym for pro-government. *Conservative* means anti-government, also pro-market, pro-business, and pro-private enterprise.

These redefinitions are recent, yet rarely examined and routinely expanded. Some liberals seem to believe that every problem requires a government program. Some conservatives insist that private is good, public is bad, and government should be privatized. Politicians wear labels as logos, and wield them as swords and shields.

Our laws are tainted by pay-offs and trade-offs. Special interests fund political campaigns, hire former officials as lobbyists, and draft the bills that become our laws. Laws, rules, and regulations are hundreds or thousands of pages, dense legal or technical jargon, incomprehensible to anyone who's not an expert. The complications, in part, help politicians hide their collusion with special interests, and help special interests hide their roles and the rewards they'll reap.

Our elections are mostly marketing. Politicians and policies are sold like toothpaste and breakfast cereal, and political marketing is a multibillion-dollar industry. But unlike toothpaste and cereal, which are tested, regulated, and come with a list of ingredients, political products lack disclosures and can be noxious or toxic.

Our elected officials are, no surprise, politicians. Did something good happen? They'll take credit. Anything bad? Their opponent's fault entirely. Ask a question, and they respond with scripted sound bites and talking points. If they say something often enough, they seem to believe, it must be true or will somehow become true. Novice politicians are normally sincere, but most are soon infected with a virus that kills courage and replaces it with careerism, self-righteousness, and a sense of entitlement.

What went wrong? Why is the system so dysfunctional?

Many of us blame special interests. That sounds persuasive and there's plenty of evidence to support it. But it's not the whole story, obviously not, because special interests have been wielding power throughout American history. Our Constitution contains blatant concessions to a wealthy special interest: slave-owners.

Special interest has no set definition, the meaning is set by the speaker. Ask a liberal Democrat, and it refers to Wall Street, the N.R.A., oil companies, evangelicals. Conservative Republicans are likely to list Hollywood, trial lawyers, environmentalists, gays and lesbians. Independents cite from both sides, and often indict the Democratic and Republican parties. *Special interest,* to summarize, is a proxy for "powerful groups I dislike or oppose." One exception is widely praised, envied, and celebrated, an extra special special interest: the superrich.

Many blame the news media. A free press is necessary to hold politicians and government accountable, and freedom of the press is protected by the First Amendment. Today, though, "the press" and "the media" are, mainly, big companies that seek profits first, before truth. They highlight conflicts, controversies, personalities, and drama, presenting politics as a reality TV show or a spectacle. Democrats and Republicans share power, and the news media normally report two sides to each issue, those two sides, dismissing or discounting other perspectives. Big media companies are plainly biased toward their own interests, touting themselves even when reporting on their failures, as we saw in 2016, with countless stories about "news" and "fake news." Big media companies are a uniquely privileged special interest, and uniquely challenged.

Many blame social media (Facebook, Twitter, Instagram, etc.), and maybe extend the blame to include Google, Apple, Microsoft, and Amazon. The internet has severely disrupted our lives, our culture, and our politics. Before, people on the street made eye contact and said "Hi"; now many of us stare at smartphones and wear earbuds.

We're constantly in contact with friends, "friends," and newsfeeds filled with gossip, rumors, and ads, including political ads and lies. Big internet companies are a special interest with unknown, or unknowable, influence.

But blaming is misleading. Special interests are not the main cause of political dysfunction, though they clearly profit from and exacerbate it.

Public withdrawal is more fundamental. Too many of us turned off and turned away from politics. Special interests moved into the gap, extending their access, increasing their influence, procuring funds and favors, providing further reasons for regular folks to withdraw. Withdrawal, apathy, and low voter turnout are now normal and expected. Pundits lament it and academics try to explain it, while politicians count on and exploit it, with negative campaign tactics designed deliberately to drive people away.

Withdrawal has come with, or from, feeling powerless. We're also angry. Public anger ignited the Tea Party in 2009, Occupy Wall Street in 2011, and Black Lives Matter in 2013, each with a surge of rage at the status quo. Anger was a huge factor in the 2016 election. "Populists" emerged in both major parties, and defied entrenched political establishments. Bernie Sanders nearly won the Democratic nomination. Donald Trump was elected.

Trump promised to "drain the swamp," to end the decades-long cycle of failure, corruption, and special interest dealing. At rallies around the country, thousands of supporters chanted his phrase: *Drain the swamp.* Can he? Will he? We'll see.

Anger is healthy, necessary, the spark and the fuel for our efforts to repair our broken government. Yet anger is often unproductive and sometimes self-destructive. Tea Party Republicans shut down the federal government for sixteen days in 2013. Occupy activists emphasized income inequality and emboldened liberal Democrats. Black Lives Matter confronts both parties. Three distinct movements – different folks, goals, strategies, and tactics – though a common outcome: intensified political paralysis.

Political paralysis persists as a by-product of multiple groups competing for attention, privileges, and public funds. Men versus women, seniors versus youth, rich versus middle-class versus poor, urban versus suburban versus rural. Some conflicts concern race or ethnic or religious identity: whites versus blacks or Latinos or Asians; evangelicals versus Catholics or Jews or Muslims or atheists. Some conflicts focus on a single issue, such as guns or abortion. Most of the time, though, groups and issues are muddled together: tax-cutters versus environmentalists versus education reformers versus health care activists versus supporters or opponents of whatever's in the news at the moment.

If one group wins anything, other groups fight on and sometimes win the next round. In nearly all political conflicts, consequently, the real winner is the status quo. The superrich get richer and more super.

Politicians promise to unite us, work together, find the center, and transcend partisanship. But that's only rhetoric. The conflicts, competition, and conventional assumptions have us trapped. Regular folks and politicians – also CEOs, billionaires, journalists, academics, and activists – are trapped in a dysfunctional system.

The trap is partly from overlooking the different uses and meanings of *we*. When a friend says "*We* should ... ," for example, listeners can agree, "Yes, good idea." Or decline, "No, I'd rather not." Or propose an alternative, "Instead, let's ... ." The personal *we* is voluntary and mutual. The personal *we* requires consent, and true consent requires freedom to dissent or withdraw.

In other contexts, particularly politics, speakers simply assert a *we* and assume consent. Speakers say *"we* are," *"we* know," *"we* have to," etc., as if listeners already agree. Speakers presume or pretend to represent an unspecified group, *we,* as if the group is united and unanimous. Consent is contrived or imaginary; or passive, partial, fleeting, or conditional.

When regular folks use *we* this way, as an assertion, *we* is mere chatter or utter conjecture; nothing changes, there are no consequences. But *we* is different when speakers are politicians, CEOs, billionaires, and leaders of powerful groups. Their assertions and assumptions can impact countless lives. Their *we* can include or affect us without our consent, without our knowledge, or despite our dissent. Their *we* can be deceptive, coercive, completely self-serving.

The one-sided *we* is widespread, a convenient bit of public discourse, normally accepted without question. Yet *we* is also a way people avoid accountability and evade personal responsibility.

We is only valid when it's voluntary. Consent is only authentic when it's active and affirmed. Every seemingly included individual must have viable opportunities to agree or decline or propose an alternative — or there is no *we.*

Elections are supposed to express or produce a valid *we* that the public respects. But elections are blunt instruments, and in recent years have become more blunt and less respected. Many of us don't vote. Some voters select for a single issue only. Some voters are strictly against the other party or candidate. Some voters ignore issues, and choose candidates based on race, gender, religion, appearance, name recognition, or likability. Voters are often deceived or misinformed. Today, consequently, for these and other reasons, elections preclude a valid *we* instead of producing one.

A valid *we* emerges with disasters and tragedies, but the feeling is fleeting. Politicians and special interests soon politicize events, reinstating the familiar pathology. The political *we* is an assertion or assumption only, or an illusion, myth, or fraud.

There is no *we,* currently, and this is our prime challenge. Real progress requires a *we* that's meaningful, voluntary, and enduring: Meaningful for all citizens as equals. Voluntary, with active consent from a clear majority. Enduring through disasters and tragedies as well as quiet times. A meaningful voluntary enduring *we* is the key to We the People.

2. The Plan

Politics is personal, unique individuals pursuing dreams, goals, and happiness.

Politics is also social, obviously. Government is fundamentally social.

This plan respects the personal and the social. This is a way to attract, engage, and encourage individuals to actively think about ourselves as citizens. Also a way to inspire, motivate, and mobilize us to act together as We the People.

Starting with individuals, regular folks – not elites or experts, not groups or statistics or abstract ideas – this plan creates conditions for rapid progress toward realizing our ideals.

Warning: This plan is bold. More than bold, actually, it's radical; it goes to the roots, and that's the literal meaning of *radical*. Some people will object without saying why. When ideas are unfamiliar, unproved, risky, or radical, we sometimes react emotionally and swiftly say "no."

If a knee-jerk objection is your first response, please pause and exhale. We're steeped in the status quo. It colors our thoughts, feelings, and assumptions about politics and economics, and we tend to defend it even though we know it's dysfunctional. Knee-jerk responses impair our ability to think. Special interests are special-ists at jerking our knees and chains.

Bold and radical, though with many precedents. Thomas Jefferson and Thomas Paine proposed related ideas, and so did Abraham Lincoln, Milton Friedman, and Martin Luther King Jr. In 1970, mod-erate Democrats and moderate Republicans supported a prior ver-sion, the Family Assistance Plan. Most Americans favored it, opinion polls showed, and the House of Representatives passed it, twice, with majorities of two-to-one. In the Senate, however, extremes of both parties voted together, for different reasons, and outvoted the moderate supporters.

The first part of this plan is like the Alaska Permanent Fund Dividend, which has been operating since 1982. It's hugely popular. Ask any Alaskan. They love it.[*2]

The plan:

- Set an amount, say $500 or $750 or $1,000, and have government provide that each month to every adult citizen. The same amount for everyone: homeless veterans, recent graduates, working parents, retired grandparents, and the rest of us. Universal and unconditional, added to and independent of what we earn. Direct payments or factored into our taxes. A basic income, guaranteed. Citizen Dividends.[†]

---

[*] A history of related ideas, proposals, advocates, and efforts – from the Bible, Thomas Jefferson, and Thomas Paine, to the Family Assistance Plan and Permanent Fund Dividend and through to today – is in Appendix 1. Current sup-porters include prominent authors and Silicon Valley billionaires. International activities are in Appendix 3.

[†] Other names are UBI, Universal or Unconditional Basic Income; BIG, Basic Income Grant or Guarantee; Citizen's Income; Common Heritage Dividend; and Social Security for All. Proponents also use older terms, including guaranteed income, negative income tax, and Demogrants.

- Cut or eliminate programs that basic income makes superfluous: welfare, corporate welfare, and everything else that goes to a special interest or segment of the population. Many programs operate through the tax code, as credits, deductions, or exemptions, so taxes will instantly be fairer and simpler.

- Adjust the amount occasionally to relieve or prevent recessions, inflation, or other troubles, and to produce smart economic growth.

- Let state and local governments supplement it using local revenues.

Citizen Dividends will guarantee that everyone has the means to participate in markets and in politics. All of us will be on the playing field. The field will be more level, the games more fair, the outcomes more satisfying.

Basic income is the key to unlocking our political system and repairing our broken government. It opens the doors to the back rooms where special interests and political operatives hide in the shadows. When the doors are open, we can turn on the lights to see what's really going on, and why. It's also the key to restarting the engines of citizenship, reclaiming our sovereignty, and moving forward on the issues that matter to us. Every American will have meaningful incentives to work together, We the People renewed.

*   *   *   *   *

Some will say it's socialism. According to certain definitions, perhaps, though "socialism" implies a big, intrusive, autocratic government. This plan shrinks government. Compared with today, government will be smaller, less intrusive, and more democratic.

Everyone will still be free to earn as much as we can. And free to participate in markets as we choose, to spend, save, and invest as we like. Basic income repairs capitalism's flaws, saving it from itself and its excesses, to make it work for everyone.

Some will insist it's unaffordable, a budget buster. Our federal government is deeply in debt, and Citizen Dividends will cost a trillion dollars a year, perhaps two trillion or more.

Yet numerous programs will be superfluous and, unlike today, every American will have a personal stake in working together to achieve significant cuts and reforms. We'll cut welfare, end corporate welfare, close tax loopholes, and slash bureaucracies — at the federal, state, and local levels.

We can positively afford a basic income, at least a small one.

Then we'll be able to balance the federal budget and reduce the national debt. That can't happen today, and seems impossible, even though most of us want government to balance its budgets and be fiscally responsible. This plan is a crucial first step, the key to defeating the special interests that profit from the status quo.*

Some will disapprove of "something for nothing," people getting money without working and earning it. Work requirements sound like a good idea, generally, and some welfare programs require people to work. But this is not welfare. Citizen Dividends will go to full-time workers and the wealthy as well, so work requirements are unworkable.

This is about work prerequisites. Before seeking work and starting to earn, and before going to school in order to learn, people

---

* Financial matters are the subject of Appendix 2

need food, clothes, and shelter: work prerequisites, and everyone needs money to pay for them. Basic income is boots and bootstraps. Everyone will be able to lift themselves up — to live with dignity, participate in society, and climb the ladder of opportunity.

This, therefore, is not "something for nothing." This is something for being a citizen, and something that helps our whole society.

If "something for nothing" is a significant concern, we might ask everyone to serve our country in some capacity. Universal community service is an idea that liberal Democrats and conservative Republicans have supported in the past, and Citizen Dividends will make it feasible.

Some will oppose giving money to drug addicts, alcoholics, "losers," "takers," "failures." There are such people today, have been throughout history, and will be tomorrow, too, no matter what we do.

Like today, some addicts, etc., will reform on their own or with help from family, friends, faith, or therapy. Unlike today, everyone will have concrete means and incentives for personal responsibility. Folks who want to reform will be more likely to succeed.

Yes, many addicts, etc., won't change. But no matter what they do or don't do, the rest of us will be better off.

Personal responsibility is the core of this plan, and we can nurture it by linking the basic income to the justice system. When drug addicts break the law and get caught – also car thieves, con artists, corrupt CEOs; anyone and any law – courts can redirect the money to pay fines, penalties, jail fees, court costs, child support, and victim restitution. Society will have an added instrument to deter and punish wrongdoers. Individuals will have an added incentive to be responsible and do what's right.

Some will seek to exclude millionaires and billionaires. It might seem foolish to give taxpayer money to the superrich, but excluding them would require rules, regulations, and bureaucracy, with endless disputes about where and how to draw the lines. Including everyone makes sense and will save dollars. Plus, we'll simplify the tax code, eliminating loopholes, deductions, and exemptions, so millionaires and billionaires pay more than today.

The main reason to include everyone: Citizen Dividends will continuously affirm that we are citizens, each and all of us, with equal rights, equal dignity, equal liberty, and equal responsibilities.

Some will denounce it as a redistribution of wealth. Redistribution is wrong and unjust, people say; it's socialism. But government redistributes money with nearly everything it does: when it collects taxes, spends on defense, invests in infrastructure, makes Social Security payments, provides health care for disabled veterans, and so on. Our task as citizens is to insist that the taxing, spending, and investing are done well and wisely to serve common purposes. This plan empowers us to make government efficient and accountable.

Basic income is distribution, more fundamental than redistribution, and this distribution is open, equal, and honest.

At the same time, and long overdue, we'll stop the widespread – and often hidden – redistribution from regular working folks to wealthy special interests. That's beyond wrong and unjust. It's absurd.

Some will question the impact on work ethics and incentives. Basic income is just that, basic. Everyone will still have myriad reasons to work and earn: to buy a home, save for retirement, do more for our kids, pursue a romance, save for a vacation, impress neighbors or classmates or relatives, etc., our personal dreams and goals. Most of us want to get ahead, to pursue and realize our dreams, to make life better for our kids. We're ambitious and entrepreneurial and willing to work hard. As for folks whose work ethics are weak: they'll spend the money, and their spending will enrich the hardworking. Work is rewarded. Strong work ethics are rewarded.

When people are motivated by fear – or facts – of hunger, homelessness, other hardships, or debt, that's not a work ethic. That's a coercion ethic. Basic income will reduce coercion. We'll be less confused about the work ethic, the coercion ethic, and the differences between them. The work ethic will be less tainted, and therefore healthier.

Everyone will be free to seek or create work that's meaningful and satisfying. Meaningful work naturally motivates us to work harder and longer. Meaningful work is a true incentive for strong work ethics.

Some will call it an "entitlement," like Social Security, Medicare, and Medicaid. Those programs were established in 1935 and 1965, and they're very different from basic income.

This is about our unalienable rights to life, liberty, and the pursuit of happiness: entitlements endowed by our creator. Life requires food and shelter at least, and therefore money to pay for food and shelter. Without an income, life is precarious, liberty endangered, and happiness elusive. Citizen Dividends will secure every American's unalienable rights.

We are created equal, the Founders declared, and this plan enhances equality. They instituted our government to secure our rights, and this plan has government do that directly and efficiently. This appears to be a plan the Founders would approve.*

Some will worry about people being dependent on government. Welfare causes dependency, supposedly, and some people say dependency is demeaning or degrading. Dependency is definitely a concern with corporate welfare. Various special interests are parasites, living on or for government handouts.

These worries are reasons to welcome Citizen Dividends.

Welfare is necessary, today, and so is corporate welfare. There are no alternatives. Without the existing programs, many millions of us could not get by, and countless businesses would fail. There would be far more hunger, homelessness, unemployment, despair, unrest, and crime.

Basic income is the alternative. Welfare and corporate welfare will be superfluous — at least partly, and perhaps completely.

The truth about dependency, moreover, is that everyone depends on government. We all rely on it every day for our personal safety and national security. We are mutually interdependent.

Interdependence is a source of meaning and happiness, and this is self-evident in families. We experience it in sports, especially among teammates, and while cheering for Americans in the Olympics and World Cup. Also when we come together during disasters and

---

* Thomas Jefferson, before writing the Declaration of Independence, proposed giving land to propertyless individuals to secure their subsistence and their rights as citizens. John Adams asserted that "every member of society" should be "possessed of small estates" as the basis for "equal liberty." James Madison endorsed the idea of laws to "raise extreme indigence towards a state of comfort."

Endnote 1 reviews the self-evident truths in the Declaration. Jefferson wrote with editing help from Adams, Benjamin Franklin, Robert R. Livingston, and Roger Sherman, the drafting committee selected by the Continental Congress. They worked together for two and a half weeks, debating and revising the text. All five might have endorsed basic income, and perhaps the whole Congress would have.

tragedies. Interdependence is the soul of patriotism. When we salute the flag and celebrate the 4th of July, we're proclaiming our interdependence.

Citizen Dividends will recharge our patriotism. Our interdependence will be more meaningful, more voluntary, and more enduring.

Some will look at the size and scope, and see the makings of massive waste, fraud, and abuse. With basic income, however, size is a virtue; bigger really is better. An added virtue is simplicity, the fact that it's universal and unconditional.

Small programs are rarely examined. Complicated programs provide multiple opportunities to rig and exploit the system. Most programs are complicated from the start, designed by special interests that lobby legislators and capture regulators. These concerns are compounded by the proliferation of federal, state, and local programs, with their confusing or conflicting goals, rules, regulations, procedures, jurisdictions, and bureaucracies. Waste is widespread, fraud frequent, and abuse unavoidable.

Size invites scrutiny, and simplicity facilitates it. People will be watching closely, continuously, checking to be sure everything is efficient, trustworthy, and cost-effective.

If we really want to eliminate waste, fraud, and abuse, basic income is imperative.

Some will focus on what it might mean for recessions, inflation, unemployment, and economic growth. These are serious matters. When we debate the details, we'll have budgets, forecasts, and other analyses for various situations.

Economic theory supports the logic of basic income. To end recessions, for example, standard models and practices call for putting more dollars into circulation, increasing the money supply. The federal government can cut taxes or increase spending: fiscal policy. The Federal Reserve can cut interest rates, print more money, adjust bank reserve requirements, or buy government securities: monetary policy. With both approaches, the effects are delayed, uneven, uncertain. Today, though, these are the only available tools. Current policy is a two-legged stool; constant adjustments, or it falls over.

Basic income gives us a third option, a third leg to keep the stool stable. We'll end or prevent recessions by increasing the amount. People will spend the money, demanding goods and services, and our demands will drive a rapid, reliable recovery.

Inflation won't be a problem. We'll be cutting other programs, so overall government spending stays more or less constant. After we enact this plan, if there's any inflation, any time, from any cause, individuals and families will have a cushion that protects us from rising prices.

Unemployment will no longer be the major concern it is today. Unemployed folks will have money for necessities, the means to live with dignity and participate in society. The rest of us, including politicians and economists, won't be so anxious about the unemployment rate.

Economic growth will be faster, smarter, and more certain.

Some will object without saying why, no reasons, no explanations. And no alternatives, only the status quo.

When anyone objects without presenting alternatives – or calls it socialism, or says it's unaffordable, or whatever – a prudent response is to question the motives. Is the objection a knee-jerk notion? Is it self-serving? Motives matter. Objections are opportunities for special interests; delays bring in dollars.

Basic income is a way to save ourselves and our country. It may be the only way.

*   *   *   *   *

This plan, for now, is just an outline. That's on purpose. We start with dreams, goals, and values, seeking consensus on core concepts. Then we'll be prepared to debate the details.

With a core consensus, compromise will be fairly simple and straightforward. The bold common sense of this plan invites compromise by reminding us that politics is personal and compromise is in everyone's self-interest.

The sooner we act, the greater the benefits. Any basic income amount – and any details regarding program cuts, tax reforms, and so on – will free us from the trap of the status quo. Let's enact some version promptly and see how it works. Then we'll revise and improve it.

How much should Citizen Dividends be?

Our views will vary with our values, lifestyles, and circumstances: whether we're poor or rich, young or old, married or single, working or unemployed, urban or suburban or rural, parents or not, in debt or not, generous or not. The initial amount might seem too small, too large, or just right; we can adjust it after a year or two. State and local governments can supplement it from local revenues.

Say it's $500. This is a floor — solid, stable, and sturdy. No holes and no loopholes. No cracks to fall through. Each of us will get that $500 every month in addition to what we earn, money we can count on no matter what happens with our jobs, our health, our families, or America's economy. Our lives will be less stressful, so we'll be healthier; less precarious, so we'll be freer and happier.

If it's $1,000 a month, that's $24,000 a year for a couple, approximately the official federal poverty line for a family of four, two parents with two children. Citizen Dividends of $1,000 a month will end extreme poverty, as defined by the government, also ending hunger and homelessness. No other program or policy can accomplish this, nor anything close to it. We can end hunger, end homelessness, end extreme poverty — possibly within a year.

Which programs should we cut? How deeply? How quickly?

With welfare – food stamps, TANF, housing assistance, and so on – deciding may be fairly simple. Apply a classic principle, *do no harm,* and ensure that no one has a net loss. We should be extra careful about children, because child poverty is awfully high today, and about seniors and people with disabilities and special needs. A larger basic income will protect more folks, and facilitate deeper, faster cuts.

With corporate welfare – tax credits, subsidies, loan guarantees, and so on – we face real obstacles. Corporate welfare goes to special interests, and they fight for every dollar. They routinely claim that any cuts will cause a loss of jobs, or lead to higher prices, or hurt the economy, or impair economic growth, or hinder the creation of new jobs. Special interests tout themselves as "job creators," and politicians gain votes by promising us jobs. The main obstacle is our dependence on jobs.

When every adult citizen has a secure unconditional income, people without jobs will be able to get by. Special interests will lose their leverage. Thus, instead of trying to end corporate welfare bit by bit, this plan dissolves the pretexts for all of it. We can cut everything that appears to be corporate welfare, and then restore only the bits that have majority support and serve a specified public purpose.

Cutting corporate welfare, if we're serious and diligent, will eliminate a lot of wasteful military spending. That's impossible today. Members of Congress use military spending as cash cows for their districts, sacred cows that must be constantly fed, while contractors suckle and grow fat. When anyone proposes cuts or reforms, military contractors hijack the debates, wielding jobs as weapons, holding us and our security as hostages. After we enact this plan, debates about defense and security will truly be about defense and security, untainted by efforts to create jobs. We'll save money. America will be more secure.

Three programs we have to cut or reform – have to because they're unsustainable, but can't cut due to political disputes – are Social Security, Medicare, and Medicaid. Reform will be vastly easier than today. Seniors will be more secure, with Citizen Dividends added to Social Security. With this new financial bond between seniors, their children, their grandchildren, and society as a whole, everyone will have renewed reasons to compromise. Medicare and Medicaid costs will fall, perhaps substantially, because we'll have less stress and fewer stress-related illnesses.

We'll also cut federal, state, and local government spending on buildings, maintenance, office supplies, salaries, and everything else. Everyone, including government workers, will have a direct stake in making and keeping our government lean, efficient, and accountable, more like successful private businesses.

*   *   *   *   *

This plan is a bridge across the divide between liberal Democrats and conservative Republicans. Our bridge, wide and sturdy, so everyone can embark from wherever we are. Once we're on the bridge, we'll see that the divide was exaggerated, an artifact of old politics. Good people live on both sides. There's common sense on both sides — common concerns and interests as well.

Actually, it's more than a bridge; it leads to a better place. Regardless of which side anyone is on or from, we'll all be moving forward to a place that's better for everyone.

Politicians routinely promise to unite us. This plan does: liberal Democrats with conservative Republicans, the Tea Party with Occupy activists; also moderates, independents, conservatives who are not Republicans, Democrats who are not liberals, Greens and Libertarians and members of other "third" parties, and folks who are usually apolitical or antipolitical. We'll dissolve the old divisions, definitions, and identities, and transcend the politics of us versus them. With this plan there's only us, each of us and all of us. Everyone will have reasons to act together as We the People.

When we consider the details, we should start by simply stating our personal preferences. What do I want? A large basic income, or fairly small? Deep cuts to welfare, or extra careful? Rapid reforms of other programs? We'll have to compromise, and compromise will be easier when we shed, avoid, or transcend political labels. While talking with other folks, ideally, we won't ask, won't tell, and won't care about partisan identities or political ideologies. Keep it personal.

Elected officials who endorse this plan will be displaying real courage, risking loss of support from the special interests that helped them get elected. True leaders will craft successful compromises, plus effective ways to educate folks.

"I promise to put people first," politicians proclaim. "My goal is to empower people." This plan does both, putting us first and empowering us directly, concretely, with cash. Politicians who campaign for basic income will prove that they're sincere, that they truly care about individual citizens. And that they trust us — real people, unique individuals, not "people" as a rhetorical device or a euphemism for special interests.

On nearly every issue – unemployment, education, global warming, health care, etc. – Republicans say the market has to provide solutions, while Democrats assert the need for government programs and regulations. Both sides overlook the obvious facts: markets and government are created by, and consist of, individuals. Individuals are first.

Individuals gain economic security with this plan, and We the People regain our sovereignty. Security and sovereignty — and synergy, markets and government working together to enrich all of us. This plan will:

- end hunger, homelessness, and extreme poverty.
- make the tax system more fair, simple, and sensible.
- improve health, and yield better healthcare at lower cost.
- decrease crime, and promote cost-effective criminal justice.
- facilitate market-driven progress on pollution and global warming.
- revitalize cities and towns, making them more distinct and attractive.
- encourage prudent immigration policies, good for citizens and businesses.
- generate a surge in small businesses forming and growing and creating jobs.

- expedite education reforms that work for students, parents, and communities.
- enhance local, state, and federal government efficacy and accountability.
- lead to enduring national security.

These gains are readily attainable. Basic income, in part, pays us to participate as citizens. We'll be paid for cooperating and compromising.

Progress starts with us, our personal dreams and goals.

*   *   *   *   *

What do you think?

Would you like a basic income added to what you earn?

Should it be $1,000 a month? More? Perhaps $750? Less? Only $500 a month?

To get the money – every month, guaranteed, for the rest of your life – here are three things to do:

- Agree to have every adult citizen get the same amount. Everyone — unless a court redirects funds for some purpose, such as to pay a fine or child support.
- Tell your friends, neighbors, co-workers, and other folks about this plan. Ask them to join you in attracting and educating more supporters.
- Demand that politicians make this their top priority, and that they compromise on the basic income amount, program cuts, tax reforms, and other details.

You might get Citizen Dividends soon, possibly this year. You and your family, your friends, your neighbors, and so on.

Imagine what you could do with the added income. If it's $1,000 a month, that's $12,000 a year. For you and a spouse, $24,000. Consider the possibilities, your dreams, goals, values, and overall quality of life.

Are you unhappy with your job? Most of us are, or say we are. Are you unemployed or underemployed? You'll have a secure income while you pursue happiness. If you don't know what to do, or you need specific skills or a degree, you'll have money for education. Is there work you'd like, but it has low pay, such as teaching? You might view basic income as a salary supplement. Is your job okay, but only okay? You'll have leverage, an independent income, when you ask for a raise. Want to start your own business? You'll have a launch pad.

You might choose to be a full-time parent. Move closer to a job, your kids, your parents, or just someplace new. Pursue creative interests as a writer, artist, musician, or inventor, whether as a profession or simply for the joy of learning. Travel. Develop hobbies. Devote more time to volunteering in your church or community activities.

Are you caring for a spouse or parent with Alzheimer's, cancer, MS, or after a stroke? A warrior who was wounded in Iraq or Afghanistan? A child with autism or cerebral palsy? You may be the one who's receiving care. Caregivers endure immense stress and constant challenges. This added income, perhaps $2,000 a month for you and your loved one, can make a huge difference.

If you're concerned about people misusing the money, is it anyone in particular? An alcoholic co-worker, a neighbor who abuses pain pills, a nephew obsessed with online games, someone you saw on the street? Yes, some folks will misuse the money, yet they'll have the means to change if they choose. When folks need extra assistance, their friends and family will have greater means to provide it. You might offer to support someone you care about.

Have you ever dreamed about doing something significant? Are you willing to serve your community actively? You can join or start a group that's working to enact Citizen Dividends, or perhaps run for public office. You can help make history.

As you pursue your dreams and goals, other folks will be pursuing theirs. From our personal actions, a unified outcome — a freer, stronger, healthier, and more democratic America, and a more peaceful world.

3. To Make Taxes Fair and Simple

With this basic income plan, we can have a tax system that's fair, simple, sensible, and consistent with our goals and values.

Taxes today are an abomination. That's a consensus opinion, one of the few bits of real political consensus, and it's more than an opinion. According to the Taxpayer Advocate Service, an independent organization within the Internal Revenue Service, taxes are "a significant, even unconscionable, burden." Individuals and businesses spend 6.1 billion hours every year on filing our taxes, and that's equivalent to more than three million people working full-time, year-round.[3]

Every taxpayer loses a few of those 6.1 billion hours – some lose dozens of hours – and most of us spend money on tax preparation software or an accountant. That's our time and our money, and government is taking them from us. What are we getting in return? What does the tax code produce? Anger and resentment, fraud or temptation for fraud, slower economic growth, struggling or failing businesses, and a bloated dysfunctional government.

The tax code is wicked for the usual reasons. It was designed by and for special interests. Every complication is a confection, a load of sugar that keeps some groups fat and happy, though alert and sometimes hyperactive. Any hint of reform, and special interests transform into black-belt defenders of the status quo.

Politicians routinely promise to simplify the tax code. They sound sincere and perhaps they are, but their top priority is getting elected or reelected. Most "reforms" are only rhetoric or campaign fodder, red flags to attract attention, red meat to reward selected donors. "Tax reform" is a racket.

The racket rests on two tenets – taxes are bad, tax cuts always good – but both are flawed. Taxes pay for government services we depend on, and will fund our Citizen Dividends. Tax cuts mainly go to special interests; good for them, obviously, and good for the politicians who get to proclaim themselves tax-cutters and reformers. Too often, however, government is left without funds for essential services — and that's bad for everyone.

This plan ruins their racket. We'll take away the politicians' toys, and end the games they play with our money.

*   *   *   *   *

How should we fund our government? What taxes make the most sense? Let's consider some possibilities:

A flat income tax: The concept is simple. Eliminate loopholes, deductions, and exemptions, and have everyone pay the same rate. State your income, multiply by the set rate, and that's what you owe. "Tax forms that fit on a postcard." Proponents also want to broaden the tax base, so more folks have a direct stake in our government — shared sacrifice, skin in the game.

But it's not fair. People with low and moderate incomes spend every dollar just to get by, so job losses, illnesses, accidents, and other setbacks can be devastating. The rich have resources to recover from setbacks, and money to invest in their efforts to get richer. A flat tax is a recipe for rising inequality.

A progressive tax code – higher rates on higher incomes – has been a core principle since the income tax began in 1913. In the 1950s, there were 24 tax brackets and a top rate of 91 percent. Yet that was a time of rising prosperity for Americans. Poor folks could work hard, make it into the middle class, and possibly get rich. Everyone had a shot at winning the game.

Tax policy is a dilemma. We want taxes to be fair and simple, but these ideals seem incompatible. The dilemma affects every tax, every reform proposal, every debate about who pays for our government and who gets help from it — and therefore every question about wealth, poverty, and income inequality. Throughout U.S. history, these issues have ignited major protests, including the Tea Party and Occupy Wall Street.

The dilemma dissolves with a tax-free basic income. These four tables show a perfectly flat tax, income tax rates of 15 and 30 percent, and annual tax-free Citizen Dividends of $6,000 and $12,000:

Pre-tax Income	15 % Tax	Citizen Dividends	Net Tax	Net Income	Net Tax Rate
0	—	$ 6,000	$ -6,000	$ 6,000	—
$ 10,000	$ 1,500	6,000	-4,500	14,500	—
20,000	3,000	6,000	-3,000	23,000	—
40,000	6,000	6,000	0	40,000	0
80,000	12,000	6,000	6,000	74,000	8 %
160,000	24,000	6,000	18,000	142,000	11 %
320,000	48,000	6,000	42,000	278,000	13 %

Pre-tax Income	15 % Tax	Citizen Dividends	Net Tax	Net Income	Net Tax Rate
0	—	$ 12,000	$ -12,000	$ 12,000	—
$ 10,000	$ 1,500	12,000	-10,500	20,500	—
20,000	3,000	12,000	-9,000	29,000	—
40,000	6,000	12,000	-6,000	46,000	—
80,000	12,000	12,000	0	80,000	0
160,000	24,000	12,000	12,000	148,000	8 %
320,000	48,000	12,000	36,000	284,000	11 %

Pre-tax Income	30 % Tax	Citizen Dividends	Net Tax	Net Income	Net Tax Rate
0	—	$ 6,000	$ -6,000	$ 6,000	—
$ 10,000	$ 3,000	6,000	-3,000	13,000	—
20,000	6,000	6,000	0	20,000	0
40,000	12,000	6,000	6,000	34,000	15 %
80,000	24,000	6,000	18,000	62,000	23 %
160,000	48,000	6,000	42,000	118,000	26 %
320,000	96,000	6,000	90,000	230,000	28 %

Pre-tax Income	30 % Tax	Citizen Dividends	Net Tax	Net Income	Net Tax Rate
0	—	$ 12,000	$ -12,000	$ 12,000	—
$ 10,000	$ 3,000	12,000	-9,000	19,000	—
20,000	6,000	12,000	-6,000	26,000	—
40,000	12,000	12,000	0	40,000	0
80,000	24,000	12,000	12,000	68,000	15 %
160,000	48,000	12,000	36,000	124,000	23 %
320,000	96,000	12,000	84,000	236,000	26 %

These tables clearly show the interaction of the two variables, tax rates and Citizen Dividends. A small basic income, and the rate can be low. If we want a larger amount, we'll have to pay a higher rate. Higher rates will also be necessary if we want to pay down the federal debt, invest in infrastructure, or increase spending for national defense.

This is obviously fair, extremely simple, fully inclusive, and the net effects are clearly progressive. Every taxpayer pays the same rate on every dollar of earnings, yet high earners pay a higher percentage. People with incomes below the break-even point – in these examples, $40,000, $80,000, $20,000, and $40,000 – get payments from our government, a *negative income tax*. This tax system is easy to understand. Taxes are easy to calculate.*

Shared sacrifice and equal rewards. Skin in the game and money in our hands. The same basic income for every citizen, and the same tax rate for every taxpayer and every dollar we earn.

Both variables affect a wide range of concerns, issues, problems, and solutions. Both will be topics for elections. After elections, because this system is so obviously fair, simple, and inclusive, compromises will be straightforward.

With current efforts to reform the tax code, the burden is entirely on those who are calling for change, and the burden is heavy. This plan lifts the burden and moves it to the other side; special interests will have to carry that weight. Groups that want tax breaks will have to make their case, explain their priorities, and attain popular support.

Are there tax breaks, credits, deductions, or exemptions we should retain?

- Lower rates for capital gains and dividends? The main
  beneficiaries are wealthy investors and Wall Street brokers.

---

* *Negative income tax* is what economist Milton Friedman, a Nobel Prize recipient, called his version of basic income. He discussed it in his 1962 book, *Capitalism and Freedom,* which also proposed "a flat-rate tax on income above an exemption." Combine and streamline his proposals, and the result is somewhat like these tables.

- Interest on mortgages? Homeowners with bigger loans get bigger deductions; renters get nothing. The deduction is an indirect subsidy for the banking and housing industries. And it increases home prices for everyone.
- Deductions for children? We can help parents and their kids in other ways, by providing quality daycare, investing in early education, or with a larger basic income. Another option is to create a parallel program of universal child benefits, perhaps $200 or $300 a month for each child.[4]
- Charitable contributions? Charity is personal. Generosity is a virtue. Giving is meaningful and satisfying. We'll continue to support groups and causes we believe in, just because we care.

Some tax breaks, etc., help the poor; others aim to aid the middle class; most of the money, by far, goes to the wealthy. The current tax code fuels class warfare. This plan ends class warfare for good.[5]

Real tax cuts, not rhetoric, with lower rates for nearly everyone. Only a few people will pay more: millionaires and billionaires will lose their loopholes. Yet they'll also shed the resentment they face when regular folks hear about their tax breaks, trust funds, offshore accounts, and other privileges. The superrich might view higher taxes as a smart investment — an investment with a guaranteed positive return, a more just, stable, and prosperous America.

Consumption taxes: Many economists say we should tax spending or consumption, instead of income, to encourage people to save and invest. Saving and investing are good for individuals, families, and our society as a whole.

One way to tax consumption is to do so directly. Total income, minus savings and investments, equals spending — then pay taxes on that sum, filing tax forms like today. Rates could be flat or progressive. We could easily combine this approach with basic income. Another option is a value-added tax, a sales tax assessed at each stage in the production of goods and services. A VAT is very efficient. Economists like it because it's easy to collect and hard to avoid. Canada, England, Germany, Israel, Mexico, and other market-oriented democracies use it as their primary tax on corporations. America taxes corporate profits, not production, and that's the main reason U.S. corporate taxes are higher and more complicated than other countries. Certain politicians oppose the VAT, claiming that it would lead to bigger government. Citizen Dividends will empower us to keep government small, so a VAT might be smart politics and smart economics.

A third possibility is a national sales tax. Proponents call it the "Fair Tax," and they estimate a 28 percent rate, paid at the cash register when we buy anything. The Fair Tax would replace income taxes, payroll taxes, estate taxes, gift taxes, capital gains taxes, and corporate taxes. Paychecks would include 100 percent of pay, minus only state income taxes. To protect the poor, proponents call for a "prebate," a cash payment each month to offset sales taxes on food and other necessities. That prebate would vary with household size (single adult, couple with two children, etc.) so it's like a basic income, though more complicated.

We could have sales taxes on everything people buy online, and that would level the playing field for local merchants. Also sales taxes on financial transactions, the selling of stocks, bonds, derivatives, and such. Financial transaction taxes would be quite small, 0.01 percent to 0.5 percent, so they won't deter long-term investments, yet this would restrain high frequency trading and could prevent market crashes and meltdowns. Financial markets will be more stable, and stability is good for entrepreneurs, good for investors in start-ups, and good for everyone who's saving long-term. Many jurisdictions tax financial transactions, including Hong Kong, Singapore, and the London stock exchange.*

Carbon taxes and land value taxes: Carbon taxes – taxes on oil, coal, and natural gas, calculated on the carbon emitted when the fuels are burned – have been proposed in several states and nationally, chiefly in the context of concerns about climate change. But that context conceals the concept. More fundamentally, these are taxes on what people take from nature.

The concept is simple. Oil, coal, and natural gas are provided by nature. So are metals, minerals, air, water, timber, seafood, and much more. These are – or ought to be, at least partly – our common wealth and heritage. When anyone claims, collects, consumes, or degrades what nature provides, some fair market value can be assessed and taxed to repay the community. Taking from nature, after all, is taking from society and from future generations.†

Land value taxes are property taxes assessed on the land only, not buildings or other improvements. This is simpler than a property tax on buildings, because land is visible and measurable, while buildings depreciate and assessments fluctuate. Tax rates, ideally, are based

---

* Financial transaction taxes are sometimes called "Tobin" taxes, for economist James Tobin, a Nobel laureate. He also endorsed basic income.

† This concept inspired an early call for universal income support. Thomas Paine, in 1797, described land as the "common heritage of mankind." He wanted landowners to pay a "ground rent" into a "national fund." Every citizen would then receive a cash payment at age 21 and yearly payments starting at age 50 as "a right, and not a charity."
    Similar insights sparked the creation of Alaska's Permanent Fund, which collects a portion of oil royalties, and Permanent Fund Dividend, which distributes money to every resident. Appendix 1 has more about Alaska's PFD and Paine's *Agrarian Justice.*

on the full rental value of the land, so these taxes are incentives to use land wisely and to build wisely. In cities and suburbs, land value taxes favor compact development, neighborhoods where people walk to work and shop, instead of car-dependent sprawl. In rural areas, because town centers are more compact, land value taxes help preserve farms and protect open spaces.

Milton Friedman called this "the least bad tax," because taxing land does not reduce the supply or quantity; other taxes discourage whatever is taxed, income, labor, production, or consumption. Joseph Stiglitz – a Nobel laureate in economics, like Friedman – endorses land value taxes to reduce inequality. Wealthy people and corporations are major landowners, and they'd pay almost all of the taxes. The wealth gap is much wider than the income gap, Stiglitz notes, and this tax can shrink both.*

Carbon taxes and land value taxes are like users' fees for consuming or exploiting nature; a formal term is *economic rent*. They're also like sales taxes, although assessed upstream, at the source or site of taking something from nature, as distinct from sales taxes at the gas pump, utility bill, or cash register. Assessing taxes upstream is far more efficient.

With taxes on what people take from nature, we promote market-based progress toward environmental sustainability. Raw materials become more expensive, an incentive to innovate and be more efficient. Reused materials would not be taxed, so reuse, recycling, and redesign would be rewarded. Taxes on takings, therefore, protect

---

* An early champion of the land value tax was political economist Henry George. His 1879 book, *Progress and Poverty,* sold more than a million copies. He called for taxing land only, a "single tax," calculated to confiscate all profits from speculating on land. That would yield enough money to fund all legitimate government expenses, he asserted, plus a surplus that could be divided among the community, "share and share alike."

nature and conserve raw materials while shrinking government and promoting private enterprise.

Payroll taxes, estate taxes, and corporate income taxes: These are substantial and we have to reevaluate each of them — after we have basic income, so special interests don't dominate debates and dictate decisions.

With payroll taxes for Social Security, Medicare, and Medicaid, the reasons to wait are obvious. Current rates and programs are unsustainable, but the affected special interests are powerful and ready for battle. When seniors have Citizen Dividends, they'll be more secure. We'll have less stress and better health, therefore significantly lower costs for Medicare and Medicaid. Reform will be much easier than today.

Estate taxes only affect multimillion dollar estates – about 5,000 estates each year – after the owner's death, which is why some politicians call it the "death tax." Under a 2001 law, the rate gradually fell to zero in 2010, for one year only, then jumped back to 35 percent on estates larger than five million dollars. The superrich are again lobbying for total repeal. Class warfare? The superrich versus the rest of us? Ceasefire, please, until after we enact basic income and reform other parts of the tax code.

Corporate income taxes are complicated and the base rate in America is higher than other countries. These features are invitations to keep money abroad, to reincorporate in the Cayman Islands or other tax haven, or to buy or merge with a foreign company and avoid domestic taxes through inversion. Big corporations have big budgets for lawyers, accountants, and lobbyists who are experts at minimizing or evading taxes. They also have big budgets for public relations, to persuade us that we should cut their taxes. Corporate taxes are major considerations in foreign trade negotiations. Trade agreements and corporate tax reforms can wait. Basic income first.

Initial suggestions: A smart tax system has to respect regular folks and our everyday lives. Tax concerns should never dictate our choices about marriage, kids, jobs, where to live, or when to retire. Our choices should be truly ours and truly free, and this should be true for everyone equally, the poor, middle class, rich, and superrich.

- Tax income: Let's start with a flat tax and tax-free basic income, a simple negative income tax. After a year or two, we'll probably have to adjust the tax rate or basic income amount, and that'll be a time to reconsider and perhaps restore specific tax credits, deductions, or exemptions.

- Tax spending: Consumption taxes make sense, and we can phase them in, perhaps while cutting income taxes. Start with a VAT, like most other countries, then financial transaction taxes and sales taxes on all online purchases. To maximize efficacy and revenues, we should make it easy to coordinate local, state, and federal programs.

- Tax takings: We should periodically increase taxes on oil, coal, metals, minerals, and other natural materials, and shift property taxes off buildings and onto land values. Taxes on takings might be the main or sole funding source for local governments. Land is local, obviously, and natural materials have a local origin.

- Reevaluate payroll taxes, estate taxes, corporate taxes, and all other taxes, starting soon after we enact Citizen Dividends.

This tax system has distinct elements, explicit dynamics, and ready options for revisions. When we have reasons for further reform, the politics will be more honest than today, less tainted by biases such as "class warfare." We'll compromise.

Taxes can be fair and simple, and inclusive, efficient, and non-intrusive. Taxes can fund current activities while furthering our long-term interests. We just have to start with a tax-free basic income.

*   *   *   *   *

Do you think a flat tax makes sense?

Would you support a VAT? Fossil fuel taxes? Land value taxes? Financial transaction taxes?

Suppose the basic income is $1,000 a month, tax-free, and income taxes are perfectly flat. If you earn less than $80,000 a year and the tax rate is 15 percent, you'll get money from our government — a negative income tax. If the rate is 30 percent, you'll be getting money if you earn less than $40,000 a year. That money will arrive via your paycheck, through lower withholding, or deposited directly into your bank account.

Your paycheck will be larger than today and your taxes lower (unless you earn a huge amount and you currently utilize loopholes and deductions). Tax forms will be simple, possibly a postcard. Filing may be unnecessary, the whole process automatic.

What do you think the tax rate should be? Would you agree to 30 percent? What about 40 percent, if that's what it takes to balance the federal budget? Or should we keep it lower, say 15 or 20 percent, while using other taxes to provide additional funds?

Are there tax credits or deductions you want to preserve? For children, say, or contributing to charities? Talk with friends, neighbors, politicians, and other folks. Tell them what you think, and why. If a majority agrees, we'll keep or restore those deductions.

Now suppose we also have a VAT. And higher taxes on oil, coal, and natural gas. And land value taxes instead of property taxes on buildings. And financial transaction taxes that deter short-term speculating on stocks, bonds, currency, and such.

You can avoid the VAT by spending wisely. Avoid financial transaction taxes by investing long-term. Avoid fossil fuel taxes by working from home, moving closer to your work, commuting by mass transit or bicycle, or remodeling your home to make it more energy efficient. You might welcome fossil fuel taxes as a way to foster sustainability without additional regulation, simply through the self-interested actions of individuals and businesses.

Do you own your home? If you remodel – adding a room for an aging parent, say, or an apartment over the garage to rent out – your taxes won't go up because the land value tax is on the land only. If you move, you'll be less constrained by concerns about taxes, and more free to choose the home you want, size, style, and location, and whether to buy or rent.

Are you an employer? Self-employed? Working multiple jobs or independent contracts? Tax-filing and record-keeping will be easier than today, with fewer worries and lower costs for accounting and compliance. You'll be able to invest more time and money in building your business.

Want to start a business? You'll have plenty of options and opportunities. We'll see rising demand overall, with direct financial incentives for efficiency and innovation. That means demand for planners, designers, consultants, inventors, architects, engineers, plumbers, carpenters, electricians, and general contractors. You'll also have plenty of opportunities to invest in those companies and industries.

Are you concerned about the schools your kids attend, or about your local parks, roads, businesses, or transit options? What about clean air, clean water, and land use? You and your neighbors will have more power to influence local government, and local officials are likely to be more responsive to residents' concerns.

Real tax reform is possible. You can help make it happen.

4. To Reform and Shrink Government

Start with basic income and tax reform, and further cuts and reforms will be easy, even inevitable. Regular folks will demand smaller government, and we'll have renewed power to hold our representatives accountable — power to get the results we want.

The key to success when cutting programs – a key that would-be reformers often forget, misplace, or fail to consider – is to first make programs superfluous. We do that with Citizen Dividends. The doors will open wide to welcome changes that are currently denied.

Welfare for individuals and families: Welfare is a safety net, supposedly, but the holes are large and irregular, the material tattered and unraveling. Millions of folks are entangled in the net or trapped beneath it. Welfare is a hodgepodge of programs with onerous requirements and huge bureaucracies.

Basic income is a floor. Solid, stable, and sturdy, with no holes and no cracks. There's room on the floor for every citizen, none left outside or locked in the basement. No barriers or obstacles, no waiting in line. And because it's universal and unconditional, minimal bureaucracy.

Whether deeply and quickly or extra carefully, we'll cut, reform, or eliminate:

- TANF, the program most people refer to as *welfare*. TANF is Temporary Assistance for Needy Families, a federal program administered by the states, with rules, regulations, and restrictions that vary from state to state. Because it's temporary and only helps "needy families," every state has a big bureaucracy, with constant hassles for recipients, bureaucrats, social workers, and elected officials.

- The Supplemental Nutrition Assistance Program, known as *food stamps*. SNAP has eligibility requirements, restrictions on purchases, and related complications. These features are a burden and stigma on 43 million Americans.

- Housing assistance. The federal government has a Department of Housing and Urban Development, with similar agencies in states and cities. Housing agencies pay people's rent, own apartment buildings, and impose various restrictions on bankers, realtors, and developers. These interventions distort housing markets.

- Unemployment benefits. Multiple programs provide job-training and money to pay bills, though only for the newly-unemployed. Benefits stop after specified periods.

- Medicaid and related programs.

Various welfare programs operate through the tax code, and will simply disappear with a negative income tax. An example is the Earned Income Tax Credit. The EITC was enacted in 1975, a few years after the Senate blocked the Family Assistance Plan, which was a guaranteed income or negative income tax; the EITC was created as a fallback, compromise, or afterthought. Although it has major flaws, it's been repeatedly expanded, with bipartisan support, and now helps 30 million workers at a cost of $82 billion a year. Citizen Dividends will be far more effective and efficient.[6]

We can apply the ethical imperative, *do no harm*. With a large basic income, we'll cut programs deeply and quickly, and eliminate whole agencies. With a smaller amount, we'll have to preserve programs – at least partly – to protect kids, seniors, and people with disabilities and special needs.

If Citizen Dividends are $1,000 a month, a couple will get $24,000 a year. That's close to the official federal poverty level for a family of four, and it's much more than current programs provide to typical poor families. We'll end extreme poverty while eliminating a wide range of federal, state, and local programs.

For single parents, a portion of the absent parent's basic income could be redirected — guaranteed child support, whether voluntary or by court order. Perhaps $200 a month for each child, or $300 or $500. Various local, state, and federal welfare programs assist single parents and their kids, and we'll cut or eliminate those programs.

Another reason to enact this plan: Current programs can be "poverty traps." If participants take part-time or temporary jobs, they can lose their benefits, in some cases permanently. Most programs have residency requirements that keep people where they are, unable to relocate to places where living costs are lower, job opportunities are better, or family and friends are nearby. This plan will free everyone to pursue all opportunities.

Corporate welfare: Federal, state, and local governments give corporations many billions of dollars each year through tax credits, subsidies, loan guarantees, and such. Taxpayer money mostly goes to big companies, primarily manufacturers and real estate developers, including General Motors, Boeing, and Walmart. The stated reasons, invariably, are to create jobs and promote economic growth. The money is supposed to spill over, spread around, and trickle down. The resulting jobs and economic growth are supposed to produce higher tax revenues, so government has money for health care, education, national security, welfare for the poor, and other activities. That's the theory: corporate welfare is supposed to help everyone, indirectly.

The direct route is basic income. No waiting for money to trickle down, no praying for CEOs to spread it around. Instead, regular folks get the money and we'll spend it around. We'll demand goods and services, and companies will compete to supply them; demand-driven jobs and economic growth. Corporate welfare will be superfluous, so we can eliminate it at local, state, and federal levels.

Another form of corporate welfare, or a close relative, involves contracting or outsourcing to private companies. Such practices can be smart, sensible, and cost-effective — when the process is open and truly competitive, and when government is vigilant in supervising the procedures and outcomes. But flaws, frauds, and failures are far too frequent. Companies lobby and make campaign contributions. Contracts often appear to be, and sometimes prove to be, "pay-to-play" or "crony capitalism."

Corporate welfare and crony capitalism are cancers. From agriculture to zoos – including public safety, national security, and other core functions – nearly all federal, state, and local agencies are afflicted.

To heal the body politic, surgery is necessary. Regular folks will be the doctors, locating the tumors so our elected representatives, the surgeons, can operate. We'll also be the nurses and therapists, expediting recovery and preventing any relapse. After decades of disease and decay, America's body politic will again be healthy and strong.

Social Security: Social Security was enacted in 1935, the middle of the Great Depression. Over the following few decades, poverty among seniors declined significantly. But no longer. Millions of seniors are poor, anxious, insecure, and delaying retirement or entirely unable to afford it. Individual retirement accounts are inadequate, private pensions underfunded, and many workers lost their pensions or had them stolen when corporations went bankrupt. Fewer young workers are paying into Social Security. Americans are living longer. The current system is unsustainable.

Proposed reforms would increase payroll taxes, or raise the retirement age, or change the way payments are calculated, or lift the cap and collect more from wealthy folks, or introduce private investment options. Each proposal has champions and opponents. Special interests on every side have been preparing for years, recruiting allies, sharpening their rhetoric, and launching guerrilla attacks in Congress and through the media. The battles will be fierce, costly, and prolonged. Countless seniors will be casualties.

Or we can enact this plan. With Citizen Dividends added to Social Security, seniors will be more secure. Retirees and workers of all ages will have renewed reasons to cooperate and compromise. We'll reform the current program or replace it with something better — retirement security for seniors today, next year, and through future decades.*

Basic income is like Social Security for all — though more social and more secure. Instead of payroll taxes taken from our paychecks, money is added to what we earn. Instead of variable payments based on past earnings, the added income is equal and unconditional.

---

* The political pressure to enact Social Security came from two mass movements for guaranteed income. In 1934-5, more than two million people supported the Townsend Plan to give everyone age 60 and above a monthly payment of $200 (about $3,500 in today's dollars). Share Our Wealth claimed to have 7.5 million members, and they were demanding a guaranteed annual income for every family, $2,500 ($44,000 today).

Instead of dividing us into those who pay in versus those who get money back, we'll be united as taxpayers and as beneficiaries.

Medicare, Medicaid, and Obamacare: When basic economic security is guaranteed, we'll have less stress and lower rates of stress-related conditions (back pain, migraine, cancer, stroke, depression, sexual disorders, etc.), and therefore lower costs for healthcare.

Medicare is for seniors, and savings are sure to be substantial. Savings will increase over time because folks will be healthier when they become seniors.

Medicaid is for the poor. Poverty is a significant factor in obesity, diabetes, heart disease, and kidney disease. Even the poorest will be able to afford healthier food and regular fitness activities.

The Affordable Care Act, often called Obamacare, was designed to increase healthcare access, quality, and affordability. Citizen Dividends will advance all three goals. We can upgrade the parts that are popular, and reform or replace the rest. Subsidies will be superfluous if the basic income is adequate. Mandates and penalties might also be superfluous, because recent debates have educated everyone, including healthy young adults, about the reasons to buy health insurance. Instead of specific taxes, funds can come from user fees or general revenues. These are among the changes that Obamacare opponents – Donald Trump, Paul Ryan, et al. – have been demanding.*

---

* One version of basic income, from Charles Murray, a renowned libertarian, is $10,000 a year plus $3,000 for mandatory health insurance. He wants to eliminate Medicare, Medicaid, and Obamacare, and he views health insurance as something government can rightly require, like auto insurance. The $3,000 figure is his estimate for catastrophic coverage, with everyone free to choose comprehensive plans, employer-based programs, or health savings accounts.

Another reform option is single payer, "Medicare for All." Sen. Bernie Sanders called for that in the 2016 Democratic primaries. With Citizen Dividends and the political reforms that are sure to follow, single payer may be popular. One or two states might lead the way.

Healthcare and health insurance are extremely expensive. The money we save can cover a significant part of our Citizen Dividends.

Waste and excess in military spending: Our government spends an enormous amount on defense, the military, and homeland security. How much of that is corporate welfare? How much is crony capitalism? How much is political meddling?

Waste is sometimes obvious, but impossible to cut. When military contractors' profits are threatened, they deploy high-energy patriotic rhetoric. Our duty as citizens, they tell us, is to support the troops, salute the flag, and be proud that America is the sole military superpower. We're #1! While we're cheering and distracted, contractors are lobbying Congress, getting their requests into the budgets, and getting those budgets passed.

Military contractors and their enlisted allies – politicians, pundits, and public relations professionals – have other tactics, too, notably fear. Terrorists! Failed states! Radical Islam! Weapons of mass destruction! Our massive military is necessary, they insist, and may be inadequate unless we increase spending on drone aircraft, spy satellites, cyberweapons, cyberdefenses, and the next generation of ships, jets, nuclear weapons, and everything else. Remember 9/11!

When contractors and politicians are not sowing fear or deploying patriotism, they're talking about jobs. Military contractors constantly boast about the jobs they're creating, or tout the number that will be destroyed by any cuts. Talking about jobs is the main sign of corporate welfare. Contractors play the jobs card, and we allow it to trump other concerns.

Citizen Dividends will disarm the contractors. Americans will be more united in our patriotism, more engaged as citizens, and consequently more prepared to evaluate our true defense and national security requirements.

We'll have the military we need, without the waste. We'll be safer, because waste and excess involve more than money; there's also wasted time and attention. Our security depends on leaders who are focused, engaged, and thinking strategically about real threats. When we cut superfluous programs, we also eliminate burdens and distractions. Cutting waste and excess, therefore, is a way to support our troops.

Our security requires more than a strong military. America is vulnerable in various ways: the national debt, budget deficits, trade deficits with China, fragile global supply chains, decaying infrastructure, and our dependence on fossil fuels. Hostile nations, militant Islamists, and domestic terrorists can exploit these vulnerabilities.

Threats provoke higher spending. Spending causes debt and deficits, which deepen dependency, divide us politically, and create openings for attackers. The dangers increase year-by-year, a vicious cycle fueled by fear, fanaticism, and profit-seeking.

With Citizen Dividends, we can escape the vicious cycle and embark on a virtuous spiral. We'll be more economically secure and politically united, therefore more ready to respond effectively to any and all threats. We'll also be prepared to focus on our true goals: peace, justice, and freedom. America can lead the world toward real enduring peace.

Initial suggestions: Instead of arbitrary goals, this plan starts with real people. Every American will have reasons to demand lean, efficient, effective government. We'll eliminate some programs entirely. Other reforms should, and will, be gradual.

- Welfare for individuals and families: With *do no harm* as a core principle – and extra care about kids, seniors, and folks with special needs – let's cut deeply at the federal level, while ensuring that local programs have adequate funds and flexibility.
- Corporate welfare: A lean, efficient government, by definition, has no excess jobs. Let's examine every government program to be certain it serves common goals, not special interests. To stop crony capitalism, we must demand open, competitive bidding on government contracts, with strict oversight and penalties for violations, penalizing both the politicians and their corporate cronies.
- Social Security: We should postpone reforms until we have Citizen Dividends. Seniors will be more secure, all Americans more united, so reform will be relatively straightforward.
- Medicare, Medicaid, and Obamacare: People will be healthier and healthcare costs lower. Everyone will have money we can use for health insurance, co-pays, health savings accounts, and such. Reform? Repeal? Replace? After we enact this plan, we'll be prepared to keep calm and move forward.
- Waste and excess in military spending: Our security is paramount, and should never be compromised by efforts to create jobs. Let's act quickly to eliminate military cronyism and corporate welfare, while we focus on our true defense and security needs.

There's more, of course, much more. We'll cut or reform farm subsidies, education programs, regulations on small businesses, etc., on the federal, state, and local levels. And we'll regularly reexamine every government agency and program, seeking further cuts and efficiencies.

Citizen Dividends, plus real tax reforms and vigorous efforts to cut and reform government — a peaceful democratic revolution to free ourselves from the special interests and the status quo. It starts with us, our personal dreams and goals. And we can start now.

* * * * *

When you think about cutting government, what are your priorities?

Are there programs you want to eliminate immediately? Programs you want to protect or preserve?

Many of us seek cuts as a matter of principle; we sincerely believe in small government. Many mainly want lower taxes. What about you? Both reasons? No matter who we elect, however, and no matter what we do to force our demands, government seems to get bigger and more intrusive.

With any basic income, numerous programs will become superfluous. And everyone will have incentives to work together, to demand and get real cuts.

Have you ever used food stamps, TANF, or unemployment benefits? If you've been there and done that, you know what it's like and how it feels. Current and former recipients may have good ideas about how to cut programs while protecting children, people with disabilities, and other vulnerable folks.

How do you feel about corporate welfare and crony capitalism? Frustrated? Angry? Disgusted? You're in good company. Most of us want to eliminate that spending, at least cut it substantially, and we'll have the power to enact those cuts.

Can you see how this will help us reform or replace Social Security, Medicare, Medicaid, and Obamacare? Americans of all ages, incomes, and health conditions will have less stress — possibly a lot less. You'll sleep better at night, probably eat better and healthier. You'll also have more opportunities for healthy physical activities. Reforms are necessary in any case, and will be a lot easier after we have Citizen Dividends.

Are you a veteran? On active duty? Especially concerned about national security? A "budget hawk" who hates wasteful military spending?

If there are specific programs you want to eliminate – or reform, protect, or expand – you might run for public office. Serving as an elected official is likely to be far more satisfying than today.

We the People can have a government we're pleased with and proud of — lean, efficient, economical, and truly accountable.

5. To Produce Smart Economic Growth

When every citizen has a basic income, we'll also have economic policies that make sense to regular folk and that work for regular folks.

Unemployment: Fear of unemployment is insidious, a serious and pervasive fact of politics, economics, and everyday life. Most of us are afraid of losing our jobs. Unemployed folks are afraid they'll never find jobs. Rich folks are afraid of high unemployment causing unrest, instability, and loss of income from investments. Elected officials are afraid of losing the next election, losing their jobs, if unemployment rises.

Our fears are often tinged or merged with other feelings: shame, scorn, and stigma among or toward unemployed folks; blame and anger, particularly when politicians denounce the unemployed as losers, takers, failures, or parasites; and hypocrisy about our feelings and judgments.

Basic income will ease our fears. Because it's universal and unconditional, it'll dissolve the shame, scorn, stigma, blame, and anger. We'll be less judgmental and less hypocritical. Unemployed citizens will be regular folks.

Two frequent questions or concerns: Will people quit their jobs? What if unemployment goes up?

Work will still be a source of pride, meaning, and dignity, and nearly everyone will still want more money. People who quit jobs will seek better ones. Some will start businesses or go back to school. Some will become artists, writers, or inventors, and perhaps they'll create something unique and valuable, even world-changing. Many will be more engaged as parents.

When unemployment is voluntary, it ought to be valid. When people quit jobs to pursue dreams and goals, we normally respect, admire, and encourage them. When people start businesses, go back to school, or decide to be full-time parents, their choices will be good for our economy and our society. Will some folks misuse the money and squander their lives? Yes, some will. But they'll have an income for food and shelter, so they won't be an added burden on the rest of us.

Employers will benefit, clearly. Start-ups and small businesses will benefit the most, and they're the businesses that create the most jobs. Many employers only want, or can only afford, part-time workers or independent contractors, and there'll be many workers who prefer and seek those positions. Workers who choose full-time jobs will truly be choosing, and are likely to be loyal, motivated, and productive.

The unemployment rate will fall. The official rate, the number that's so often in the news, only counts people who are actively looking for work. When folks aren't looking, they're not counted. The unemployment rate will be merely a number, not a major public concern or political issue.

Inflation: Inflation is low when unemployment is high; there's a ready supply of available workers, so folks with jobs are afraid to ask for more money, and businesses rarely raise prices. Inflation is likely when unemployment is low; workers are in demand and emboldened to ask for higher pay, so businesses can or must raise prices. Inflation frequently fuels further inflation, a vicious cycle. Then, because politicians are afraid to act, the Federal Reserve has to raise interest rates; inflation comes down, unemployment goes up.

This plan dissolves those difficulties. Inflation and unemployment won't be so entangled. The Federal Reserve won't be so empowered.

Basic income won't cause inflation. We'll be cutting other programs, so there's no net increase in government spending. After we implement it, individuals and families will have a cushion that protects us from inflation, any time, any cause or reason.

Economic conditions will be more stable. Stability helps individuals, families, and businesses plan our lives and manage our money. It helps entrepreneurs and investors anticipate market conditions, and it helps government agencies balance their budgets. Stability is good for everyone except speculators. Speculators profit from instability and compound it. When speculators buy or sell stocks, bonds, currencies, commodities, companies, or land, the disruptions can force companies to close plants, fire workers, or declare bankruptcy. Economic instability often leads to social and political instability, sometimes to riots, famines, and wars.

For greater benefits – regarding inflation, unemployment, and overall economic stability – we can partly fund Citizen Dividends through taxes on takings, particularly fossil fuel taxes. With small increases at regular intervals, fuel prices will be predictable. Predictable higher prices are preferable to unstable low prices. Today, fuel prices fluctuate, sometimes wildly. Any change – up or down – disrupts markets and affects all economic activities. Predictable fuel prices will facilitate planning, budgeting, investing, and innovating for sustainable economic gains.

Recessions: The proper policy response to recessions, economists tell us, is to increase the quantity of money being circulated, the "money supply." Two options are fiscal policy and monetary policy. Fiscal policy includes tax cuts, subsidies, and government spending, like the Bush tax cuts in 2001 and the Obama stimulus in 2009. Monetary policy operates through the Federal Reserve, which can cut interest rates, issue more currency, buy or sell government securities, and adjust bank reserve requirements.

With both supply-side interventions – fiscal policy and monetary policy – CEOs, consultants, and lobbyists are paid first and typically paid well, before there's any increase in hiring or wages. That's what happened under Bush and Obama. Stock prices went up and Wall Street prospered while government debt and deficits deepened, income inequality widened, and most Americans were left behind.

This plan gives us a third option. We'll end or prevent recessions by increasing the basic income, either ongoing or as a one-time supplement. Regular folks will spend the money, demanding goods and services, delivering a demand-driven recovery.*

This demand-driven option is clearly distinct from supply-side policies: Money will flow upward, like from a spring, versus trickle-down from "job creators." Our government will aid citizens directly versus indirectly through banks and other big corporations. The Federal Reserve will fine-tune economic conditions versus controlling or dominating our economy.

Recent decades have been marked by recurrent recessions, continuing uncertainty, and rising income inequality — strong evidence,

---

* This approach was tested and proved effective, though in limited ways, in the recessions of 2001 and 2008-2009. The first Bush tax cut featured a one-time-only direct distribution through checks for $300 to every taxpayer. The Obama stimulus put extra money in our paychecks through a change in Social Security payroll tax withholding; workers got up to $2,200 a year for a few years. Appendix 1 reviews both programs.

perhaps proof, that supply-side policies are flawed. Demand-driven alternatives are smart, overdue, and imperative.

Economic growth: Growth is good, we're often told. More than good, growth is necessary to create jobs and generate tax revenues — unless it's too fast and leads to inflation.

Economic growth normally refers to gross domestic product, GDP, which represents the total dollar value of everything that's produced or sold in a country. Add up all the goods and services, and that's GDP. A higher GDP supposedly indicates greater overall prosperity.

But GDP measures quantity only, not quality. It disregards whether products are essential or useless, helpful or harmful, good or bad. It counts war, waste, crime, and pollution as positive line-items, as if more is better. And it spurs excess government spending. Elected officials spend our taxpayer dollars on bridges to nowhere, high-speed trains that never run, and military equipment the Pentagon doesn't want or need — then politicians claim credit for economic growth. Those claims help them get reelected, rewarded for wasting our money.

Indiscriminate or haphazard economic growth is degrading our society and destroying our planet. It's a cancer. When cancers grow, they're feared, not cheered. Yet politicians are cheerleaders for GDP growth.

Economists acknowledge these flaws. Simon Kuznets created GDP as a tool for measuring and comparing national policies, and was honored with a Nobel Prize, yet he objected to using it as a goal. Economists have developed alternative indicators, counting only what we desire, what's good, while discounting or subtracting the bad and undesirable. Various cities, states, and foreign countries use or are considering the alternatives, but GDP has a stranglehold over current policies.[7]

Smart growth is qualitative, and Citizen Dividends will enhance everyone's quality of life. Regular folks will have more money to spend, and our spending will accelerate the transition to smarter, more sustainable policies — while also increasing GDP. Economists can then use GDP as intended: a measuring tool, not a goal.

Private enterprise: People pursue self-interests. Prices are set by supply and demand. Markets are self-regulating, as if guided by an "invisible hand." Markets are most efficient when free from government interference. These doctrines guide our everyday lives and our national economic policies, and they come from the book that established modern economics, *The Wealth of Nations* by Adam Smith, published in 1776.

The market Smith described, analyzed, and praised was like a farmers market or neighborhood crafts fair. Choices were limited. Buyers and sellers interacted face-to-face. Goods and services were mostly local, and produced by the sellers. Participants lived in the community, so everyone had ongoing incentives to be fair and honest. Everyone also had roughly equivalent information about the participants and their products.

Today we pay with credit cards and have the same vast array of choices wherever we live. Faceless corporations make and sell the stuff we buy, using parts and people in multiple countries. Even our food comes from far away, via corporations that grow, process, transport, and sell it. There's far too much information to take in, and nearly all of it is biased, distorted, or manipulated for commercial purposes.

Smith's "invisible hand" was a network or system of real people with real hands. People need air, water, food, sleep, shelter, clothing, occasional healthcare, and community with other folks. We are limited by our innate needs. We are self-regulating.

Corporations seek profits 24/7. They lack innate needs and limits. They don't self-regulate, and can't. Smith never considered anything like Walmart, Amazon, or Bank of America.

Our government has a duty to protect our personal safety and to promote the general welfare — and therefore it also has a duty to regulate corporations. Modern markets require a hand that's visible and sometimes firm: the hand of government.

Efficient, fair markets – "free markets," some say – only exist when a democratic government maintains the market. Unregulated markets are neither free nor fair. When markets are unregulated or badly regulated, powerful participants can coerce, collude, conspire, fix prices, and form cartels or monopolies. These behaviors are routinely dismissed as "market failures," but that's an excuse or denial. *Market failures* are actually government failures — signs that it failed to regulate effectively.

Rules and regulations reassure us, promoting trust, consumer confidence, and business confidence. We also need referees. When companies violate rules and regulations, referees have to step in and stop them. Referees are far more important in business competitions than in football, tennis, and other sports. In business, the outcomes affect people's quality of life — and sometimes life itself, if food, shelter, or medical care are unavailable or unaffordable.

For several years prior to 2008, the laws, rules, and regulations in the banking and mortgage industries were flawed, and the referees' eyes were shut or blinded by ideology. The result: banks collapsed, stock markets plunged, General Motors and Chrysler filed for bankruptcy, and many millions of Americans lost our homes, jobs, and savings. We also lost trust in government. Our loss of trust was compounded when government "rescued" Wall Street. Finance corporations created the housing bubble and caused the collapse — and then they got an $800 billion bailout from the federal government and $4.1 trillion from the Federal Reserve. At each stage – the bubble, the collapse, and the bailout – millions of regular folks were harmed, while a few of the superrich got richer.

With Citizen Dividends, we'll have the power to demand – and get – smarter laws, rules, regulations, and referees, with effective enforcement. If the finance industry has or causes problems, we'll boost the basic income to bail out regular folks, not banks. Wall Street will be more likely to work with and for Main Street.

After the economic collapse of 2008, Congress passed the Dodd-Frank Law to regulate the finance industry. Since then, however, finance corporations have gotten bigger and wealthier – some are still "too big to fail" – and they're lobbying aggressively to weaken or repeal the law. In other industries, also, big companies are getting bigger, hiring lobbyists, and seeking deregulation. But when any company gets too big and too powerful, it threatens our democracy and our personal liberty. Our government must regulate big corporations.

Regulations ought to be clear, simple, and consistent. We might have distinct levels of regulations based on the entity's size: minimal for start-ups and small businesses, mid-size when companies cross specified thresholds, and full-on vigorous oversight for corporations that operate internationally. Plus extra supervision and controls over finance companies and the information industry; this is crucial because their transactions are ephemeral, bits of data exchanged electronically.

One way to simplify or rescind regulations is to reform the tax system. Taxes are invisible hands, ideally; regulations are like fists. Financial transaction taxes restrain speculators and promote long-term investments, so there'll be fewer reasons to regulate Wall Street. Taxes on takings – oil, coal, land, minerals, and so on – make natural materials more expensive; companies profit from curtailing consumption, so environmental regulations may be superfluous.

Private enterprises will be freer and more likely to prosper.

Economic discourse: When economic policies fail, the flaws and errors often involve abstract language.

Consider *the market,* as in *"the market* tells us" and "let *the market* decide." These phrases disregard differences between participants, particularly the distinction between people and corporations. *The market* is an aggregate, and it mainly aggregates and represents the actions, desires, interests, and intentions of wealthy people and big companies. Regular folks are insignificant, except when large numbers act in common. Poor folks are excluded almost entirely. *The market* also obscures the differences between local shops, farmers' markets, Walmart, and the New York Stock Exchange.

Consider *the economy.* The phrase is a fiction, a full-blown abstraction, an amalgam of GDP, other statistics, and the speaker's biases. *"The economy* is weak" or strong or growing or struggling, economists state, as if they're talking about something that's alive, like a person. "We have to do what's best for *the economy,"* politicians proclaim, as if this fiction is sovereign. *The economy* creates or kills jobs — a god-like creature we must serve, perhaps worship, or risk being condemned to unemployment, inflation, a recession, or worse.

In sentences that start with *"The market"* or *"The economy,"* the abstract term is the subject or agent that acts on whatever follows, the object. That object is often us, regular folks. Such statements imply that people are passive and powerless, uniform and unchangeable.

Abstract language is dangerous. Words can be vague, ambiguous, metaphor, or metonymy, yet we normally assume everyone uses words the same way. We also assume or pretend we know what people are saying, even though nearly everyone is sometimes or habitually careless, sloppy, or lazy with our language. Abstract language lulls us into complacency, often into errors or failures.

We are citizens, though we mostly behave as consumers, customers, clients, critics, spectators, or bystanders. We individuals and We the People must remember that it's *our economy,* that we participate in *our markets,* and that we are sovereign over *our government.*

Initial suggestions: Economic policies ought to focus on regular folks, always, seeking to improve our everyday quality of life and our future prospects. Smart growth is qualitative, as distinct from quantitative GDP growth.

- Unemployment, inflation, and recessions: Let's promptly implement the core plan, the negative income tax. Economic conditions will be reasonably stable, through adjusting the basic income, the tax rate, or both. For greater stability, we should reform all tax policies, and gradually increase taxes on oil, coal, and other takings.
- Economic growth: We have to pursue growth in desired activities only, while reducing or preventing whatever is

wasteful or unproductive. Let's question GDP and claims based on it, and encourage economists to continue working on alternative indicators. Let's also insist that politicians and journalists use those alternatives.

- Private enterprise: To protect people, families, and communities, and to create a level playing field for start-ups and small businesses, government has to regulate corporations appropriately. For efficient fair markets, we should demand regulations that are clear, simple, and consistent, augmented with smart taxes on takings and consumption.

- Economic discourse: When politicians use abstract terms – *the market, the economy,* and *economic growth* in particular – we should confront them. And if they can't or won't be concrete and specific, we should vote against them.

We'll have fairer markets, freer enterprises, and economic growth that's truly smart.

* * * * *

Do you often think or worry about economic issues?

Are current practices working for you and your family?

If you're confused, upset, angry, or simply turned-off, your feelings are valid and you're not alone. Economists and politicians routinely present themselves as experts, and sometimes assert that these issues are too complicated for us regular folks to understand. The so-called experts are wrong. We're smart enough. And we're citizens. If elected officials can't or won't explain issues clearly and accurately, we should elect smarter officials.

Suppose you have a basic income of $1,000 a month, tax-free, and income taxes are completely flat, say 20 or 25 percent. Also suppose fuel prices are predictable, with periodic small increases to reduce fluctuations and instabilities.

Regarding unemployment, you'll have less fear of losing your job, and more freedom to seek or create meaningful work. Regarding inflation, you'll have money to save or invest, plus a direct personal stake in policies that promote stability. Regarding recessions, you'll be more secure, with less concerns about a collapse, partly because our government will have reliable ways to stimulate economic growth and recover rapidly from any downturns.

Budgeting and managing your money will be simpler than today, and that'll help you make good decisions about a job, college, a career, where to live, and when and how to retire. When you experience any setbacks, or if you simply change your mind, you'll have a secure income and therefore multiple options.

Do you have a job you like, or that at least suits you? Your job will probably be more secure, because economic conditions will be more stable. When it's time for a vacation or family leave, or in any emergency, your boss will likely be able to find someone who's only looking to fill-in temporarily. If you want a raise or flexible hours, your independent income will give you leverage when you negotiate.

Do you own a business or want to start one? Starting and running a business will be simpler than today, because market conditions will be more stable and fuel prices more predictable. Hiring is likely to be easier. You and your prospective employees will have options for trial periods, internships, and such, to see if the job is a good fit for both of you. You'll also have more flexibility overall, because many workers will prefer to be part-time or on variable schedules, perhaps as independent contractors.

All of this also applies to your spouse, kids, parents, and friends. Their greater economic opportunities will enhance your happiness and quality of life.

Are you tired of politicians' empty promises? Turned off by their vague, abstract, or unsupported claims? You might try to educate them. Or shut them up, shut them down, and shut them out by running against them and winning.

6. To Promote Justice and Personal Dignity

Justice and personal dignity are enduring ideals, and basic income will make them more real.

Equal rights, equal treatment, equal opportunities, and rule of law are core values for democracy. Justice is also a core religious value, along with mercy and charity. Through our efforts to enact this plan – and beyond that, with our coming success – we'll fulfill secular goals and sacred duties.

Dignity, equality, and social justice: Basic income is a baseline of dignity and equality. We'll be together on the economic and political playing field; on the social, cultural, and educational playing field as well. The games will be more fair, the outcomes more meaningful.

Many of us are not in the game or even on the sidelines. We're only spectators, sitting in the stands or watching on TV. Some of us miss the game entirely, too busy or too tired from working two or three jobs. Meanwhile, fortunate folks are making plays and scoring points. The superrich act like they own the playing field, and perhaps they do. Big corporations have their names on the stadiums.

Inequality leads to indignities and injustices, perhaps inevitably. Over the past few decades we've seen a steep increase in income inequality. Charts, graphs, and animations show the huge gains made by the top 1 percent and 0.1 percent, and the stagnant or falling incomes of the bottom 90 percent. Statistics are abstract, however; personal experience is more persuasive. Each of us knows how much money we have, or how little, and how much we owe on our credit cards, student loans, and mortgages. Most of us are struggling and we know it.

When we feel poor or insecure, or abused or exploited, it's normal to seek explanations and occasionally to blame other people. Blaming is biased, typically, often based on race, gender, background, or identity. Everyone has biases. We naturally tend to trust and favor folks who are like us, and to be wary of those who are different.

This plan will enrich the poor, end tax breaks for the rich, and expand the middle class. We'll be more equal economically and socially — less blaming, therefore, and perhaps less biased.*

Justice must include everyone. When people are affected yet excluded, justice is an out-of-reach ideal. Racism won't end with this plan. Women, LGBT folks, Muslims, and other discriminated-against groups will still have to demand rights, file lawsuits, get elected to public office, and occasionally mobilize mass protests. Yet all of us will have opportunities to participate as equals in moving America forward.

Everyone will be on the playing field, at least at the starting line. Yes, some folks will still start with points on the board – wealthy parents, family connections, elite educations, great beauty – but those advantages will be less decisive. The rewards will more likely go to

---

* A national commission on poverty, equality, and social justice held hearings around the country in 1968. Members were presidents of big corporations, presidents of labor unions, prominent scholars, and politicians from both major parties, appointed by President Lyndon Johnson. Their final report was unanimous, and called for "a universal income supplement program financed and administered by the federal government, making cash payments to all members of the population with income needs."

the folks who are most creative, with real integrity and strong work ethics.

We'll see rapid progress toward true social justice — dignity and justice for all.

Crime and criminal justice: The motives for most crimes are poverty, despair, greed, and a perceived lack of options. When everyone has a basic income, every would-be criminal will have meaningful prospects for a fulfilling life. Crime will decline significantly.

Teens and young adults are the main perpetrators, and a primary factor is high youth unemployment. Another element is the desire for status. In too many places today, the only people with money are pimps, drug dealers, car thieves, and other criminals. Pimps and dealers seek vulnerable folks, give them drugs to get them hooked, then coerce them to commit crimes and prostitute themselves.

Instead, young adults will have money for school, job training, to start businesses, to start families, and to buy homes, while kids and younger teens look forward to those opportunities. Parents will have added means to guide and protect their kids, and to be good role models. Aunts, uncles, teachers, neighbors, etc., will likely be more involved in community activities. In countless ways, therefore, the whole culture will encourage kids, teens, and young adults to become good citizens.

Judges will be able to order deductions from offenders' basic income to pay fines, penalties, court costs, child support, victim restitution, and any costs for parole, probation, and electronic monitoring. When minors commit crimes, judges might deduct from a parents' basic income or defer deductions until the person is an adult. Fines and other deductions will be easy to collect and impossible to evade. Everyone – the extremely poor, the superrich, and those in between – will know that if they commit a crime, any crime, and they're caught and convicted, they'll pay for it. Effective deterrence and punishment, with minimal administrative costs.

Prisons have proliferated in recent decades, and that's partly because prisons create jobs. But keeping someone in prison costs $20,000 to $65,000 a year. We can partly cover those costs by withholding inmates' basic incomes. Then resume it when they're released, so former inmates have reliable means to move on with their lives. Recidivism will plummet. Today, folks rejoin society but can't find jobs, and they know that any arrest means "three hots and a cot," government-provided food, shelter, and health care. That's a reason for recidivism, practically a reward. Instead, former prisoners will have money and dignity, so long as they obey the law.

Many crimes are victimless, such as possession of marijuana for personal use; we'll rewrite those laws. Many prisoners are immigrants, detained because they're undocumented; we'll reform immigration. Many prisoners are mentally ill, perhaps 30 percent; we'll help them instead. Friends, families, and faith groups can assist mentally ill folks with housing, managing their money, and getting appropriate treatments. Stability is a most effective therapy.

Reforms have to include corporate and white-collar crimes. For many corporations today, fines and penalties are routine costs of doing business, factored into budgets and stock prices. But some CEOs should go to prison. And some corporations deserve the death penalty, revoking their charters.

Local and state governments will save money, hundreds of billions a year nationwide. Direct savings on prisons, police, court costs, and legal fees. Indirect savings involving stress, medical care, and lost productivity, with benefits for everyone affected by any crime, including neighbors and employers.

Basic income may also be the key to preventing mass shootings. After most incidents, in hindsight, folks who knew the perpetrator recount signs of withdrawal, alienation, mental illness, or repressed rage. Incidents are often triggered by a financial setback, such as getting fired from a job. When everyone has real economic security, we're likely to be more attentive to warning signs in ourselves and other folks. And everyone will have funds to seek help. Will friends, parents, spouses, co-workers, etc., be able to find or provide help? In most cases, yes.

Preventing crime is in everyone's interest. This plan aligns our interests, our values, and our capacities to act responsibly.

Family issues and values: Most folks have strong feelings and opinions about abortion, teen pregnancy, single parenting, same-sex marriage, transgender rights, and related issues. Our passions complicate our politics.

For many Americans, *family* evokes a stereotype from the 1950's and '60s. Men worked and earned money, wives were homemakers, kids did as they were told. Immigration was mainly from Europe, and strictly limited. Abortion was illegal, period. Teen pregnancies were hidden, and often led to forced marriages. No cell phones, no computers, and therefore no sexting, no selfies, no social media. That was also a time of rising prosperity.

Our world has changed immensely and modern families vary widely. With basic income, everyone will have the means to live their values, each in their own way. Individuals and families will choose what's best today, while preserving or recovering what they value from the past. One parent might stay home with the kids, like in the

'50s, or both might work part-time. All parents will have greater opportunities to impart positive values to our kids.

Abortions and unwanted pregnancies will decline. People will be more responsible, because everyone will know there's no way to avoid paying child support. When a parent leaves, a portion of the basic income will stay behind, deducted and redirected voluntarily or by court order. If it's $300 a month, that's $64,800 over 18 years; for multiple kids, it might be $800 or $1,000 a month. Parents may be more committed to staying together with their kids. Single folks will likely be more careful, waiting to get married before having kids.

Kids will benefit immensely.*

Education and the future: Education is a social good, a family value, and an investment toward future prosperity. Politicians say it's the key to reducing poverty; they're partly right, though they routinely downplay or overlook critical facts. Education takes time before outcomes are evident – years normally, sometimes a generation – and the gains are uncertain, unequal, and often transitory.

With this plan, everyone will have money to pursue education for themselves and their kids. Other kids too, and that's crucial. America's future prosperity depends on educating all kids to be responsible members of society. No one left behind.

When politicians tout education as a way to reduce poverty, they're mainly talking about preparing people to participate in the labor force. It's about jobs. But what if there are no jobs? Or if the available jobs are unsuitable or unsatisfying?

Life is more than working and earning. Education must be more than job-training. We have to be educated to make good choices

---

* If we want to do more for kids and families, we might create a parallel program of universal child benefits, perhaps $200 or $300 a month for every child.

about which jobs to take or refuse, and, perhaps more important, to make good choices as citizens. Education, ideally, enhances our capacities to ask questions, solve problems, think creatively, communicate effectively, and continue learning throughout our lives.

Education is also about values. A core value for most Americans is personal responsibility, and basic income will be a continuing education in being responsible. When anyone wastes or misuses the money, next month will be an opportunity to do better, perhaps with support from family and friends. We can also educate kids to use their basic income wisely when they become adults, teaching them to save and invest the money, to pursue their dreams. Kids will have concrete reasons to look forward to happy, productive, successful lives.

Our lives are changing rapidly in ways we can't predict. We have to keep learning in order to keep up. Regular folks and families must be free to make our own decisions about how to educate ourselves and our kids — and these must be our decisions, not deferred or defaulted to politicians or self-proclaimed experts. This plan empowers us – as individuals, as families, and as a country – to educate ourselves and the people we care about.

Initial suggestions: With basic income as a foundation of personal dignity, every American will have the means to seek justice for themselves and other folks.*

Dignity promotes decency and respect for diversity. Justice requires us to protect the rights of minorities, including minorities

---

* Justice, dignity, and equality were values that Martin Luther King Jr. affirmed in his call for guaranteed income. "A host of positive psychological changes inevitably will result from widespread economic security. The dignity of the individual will flourish when the decisions concerning his life are in his own hands, when he has the assurance that his income is stable and certain, and when he knows that he has the means to seek self-improvement."

of one. For lasting progress on any issue, we have to consider the facts calmly, reasonably, responsibly, and respectfully — and that'll be easier when everyone's basic economic security is guaranteed.

- Dignity, equality, and social justice: Everyone – every race, gender, background, and identity – will be on the playing field. Because we tend to overlook injustices to others, and because past injustices persist as present inequities, we should actively pursue and practice reconciliation, including reparations or other remedies.

- Crime and criminal justice: As we integrate basic income with the justice system, let's examine existing laws and prior sentences, and modify them where appropriate. We should also actively help former criminals fully reintegrate into society.

- Family issues and values: Individuals and families, each in our own way, will have greater means to live our values responsibly and consistently. This baseline of equality can be a starting line toward mutual respect for people whose values are different from ours.

- Education and the future: Education reform is on everyone's agenda, it seems. Let's introduce ideas about basic income into schooling, educating kids to use the money responsibly. Let's also create diverse opportunities for adults of all ages to continue their educations for personal and career enrichment and to be thoughtful citizens.

Injustices, inequities, and indignities are common today, and impose huge costs on individuals, families, and our society as a whole. "I feel your pain," politicians tell us. "I want to help. I'm doing my best." Their best, perhaps, but we can do better.

We now have a real alternative. We can and should admit that current policies violate our values, perpetuate injustices, and diminish personal dignity.

Our sacred and secular values require us to enact basic income.

* * * * *

Do you think we have a duty to seek justice?

Are you concerned about poverty? Crime? Racism? Abortion? Education?

You might recall injustices you've experienced, witnessed, or heard about, whether blatant or subtle, recent or remote. Most of us can recount numerous incidents — particularly if you're poor, female, black, Latino, Muslim, gay, lesbian, transgender, an immigrant, etc., though wealthy white men also experience injustice.

If you're actively working for justice, you know how hard it is to make lasting progress. Do you focus on one cause or issue? Activists usually do, to sustain interest and maintain pressure on politicians. While focusing, however, activists are competing to be first in line for funds and attention, insisting that their cause or issue is most deserving. But injustice is injustice.

Imagine America when basic economic security is guaranteed, a baseline of equality for every citizen.

Do you worry about poverty or income inequality? Problems solved! We'll end – or at least greatly reduce – hunger, homelessness, and hardships due to debts and financial difficulties. And we'll make the tax system fair, so the rich pay their share. Are you concerned that folks with special needs will be hurt by program cuts? You might demand that we apply the ideal of *do no harm,* preserving programs at least in part. You might also choose to donate time or money to faith groups, charities, or on your own, providing extra assistance to folks who require it.

Are you concerned about racism or other discrimination? Have you been active on issues involving women, say, or Muslims or immigrants? We'll be much closer to achieving a truly just society that respects and values every individual. Elected officials will have to be more prepared, willing, and able to end injustices — or they'll soon be former officials.

Have you ever been mugged or assaulted? What about your friends or family members? Do you know, or know of, anyone who was raped or murdered? Pause for a moment, please, and picture a criminal, perhaps from an incident you recently read or heard about. Got it? Did you conjure up an image of a young man?

Suppose he has a basic income. And so do his friends, parents, neighbors, and every other adult he knows. Also suppose a judge can deduct fines, penalties, and victim restitution from the basic income if he's convicted of any crime; if he's a minor, his parents might have to pay. Thus: positive role models, extra incentives to obey the law, and real prospects for a satisfying future. A very different life – and world – than for young men today. Do you see that?

Millions of us have had credit cards stolen or bank accounts hacked. Does that include you or a family member? Do you know anyone who lost a home in the 2008 financial collapse? Know anyone who had their drinking water contaminated by an oil or chemical company? Today, corporations pay fines – small ones in most cases – and then get back to business. Or they declare bankruptcy, and taxpayers are stuck with cleaning up the mess, while executives are free to start over. Should we revoke corporate charters? Perhaps put CEOs in prison?

Do you know any single parents? Child support will be guaranteed, redirected from the absent parent's basic income. Everyone will know that there's no way to avoid paying it. Even teens will be more careful.

Do you have kids in school? Are you concerned, frustrated, or angry about the education they're getting or not getting? You'll have more opportunities to be informed and involved, to meet with teachers, attend afterschool events, volunteer on class trips or for other activities. You'll also be more able to consider alternatives: trade school, private school, homeschooling, or helping to start a charter school.

If you value justice, dignity, families, education, and personal responsibility, you might talk with friends and other folks about basic income. Work on political campaigns. Contribute time or money. Consider running for office. Seek justice.

7. To Enhance Liberty and Democracy

Liberty demands and depends on democracy. Democracy protects and preserves our liberty. Basic income will boost both.

When the Founders wrote that we are created equal, and that life, liberty, and the pursuit of happiness are unalienable rights, they also declared

> ... — that to secure these rights, governments are instituted among men, deriving their just powers from the consent of the governed, — that whenever any form of government becomes destructive of these ends, it is the right of the people to alter or to abolish it, and to institute new government, laying its foundations on such principles, and organizing its powers in such form, as to them shall seem most likely to effect their safety and happiness.

In the Declaration, moreover, and as a matter of logic and experience, life comes before liberty. Life requires food, clothes, and shelter, at a minimum; these are prerequisites for liberty and happiness, and we need money to pay for them. With Citizen Dividends, we reaffirm and realize these self-evident truths.

Liberty and the pursuit of happiness: One definition of *liberty* is freedom from government. This seems obvious. Government can be oppressive, undeniably, and it sometimes makes mistakes. Nearly everyone occasionally feels abused, coerced, or oppressed by government, and some folks frequently feel that.

When we're angry at or about our government, we can replace elected officials and change laws, rules, and regulations. We have that liberty and those rights. We also have responsibilities. Disobey laws, and society breaks down. Don't pay taxes, and other folks have to pay more — and those "other folks" include our children and grandchildren.

We are most free when government is good. Effective government protects us from criminals and terrorists. It builds and maintains our roads, schools, sewers, and transit systems. It issues money and enforces laws, rules, and contracts, which are crucial for justice and commerce. It also issues patents, trademarks, and copyrights, so we have extra incentives to create and innovate. And it protects us from predatory corporations: when companies sell unsafe products, defraud customers, or pollute our air, water, or land, government is our indispensible ally in seeking redress.

Liberty, therefore, is not merely freedom from government. What we want is freedom from abuses, freedom from coercion, freedom from oppression, and freedom from bad government. We want and deserve this — and we have the power to alter our government and get it.

A second aspect of *liberty* is the freedom to pursue happiness. It's about our personal dreams and goals, and whether we have meaningful opportunities to realize them.

This idea complements the first, and may complete it. Our desire for happiness is what motivates us to free ourselves from bad government. The Founders and colonists were pursuing happiness when they brought forth a new nation.

Both aspects affirm the value of Citizen Dividends. When personal liberty and happiness are threatened, thwarted, or denied, the most common causes involve money concerns or constraints. Many of us are enslaved by poverty. Basic income means real freedom for all.

Democracy and the pursuit of happiness: When we talk about democracy, what it is and why we value it, we normally restate familiar phrases: Majority rule. One person, one vote. Fair elections. Free speech. Freedom of religion. Equal rights. Equal treatment. Equal opportunities. Rule of law. Due process. An independent judiciary. Liberty and justice for all. Government of the people, by the people, for the people.[8]

These phrases are persuasive, though inadequate. To fully understand and appreciate democracy, we have to consider what it can and should be. In an ideal democracy, every citizen has equal access to government and viable opportunities to influence it. That means equal and effective opportunities to define issues, set agendas, select candidates, and influence and approve legislation. The United States is a representative democracy, a republic, so access is mostly indirect, yet equality is fundamental. Democracy must respect and protect true political equality.

Today, inequality is irrefutable. The elite few – the superrich, elected officials, celebrities, CEOs of big companies, and leaders of special interests – have immense access and influence, far beyond regular folks. In public debates about issues, agendas, candidates, and legislation, the elite few speak first, loudest, longest, and last. They also use the news media to ratify and reinforce their actions, and to tout themselves. After elections, no matter who wins, they retain their power and privileges.

America, apparently, has devolved into an oligarchy, government by the few. Or a plutocracy, government by the rich.

We have the right to alter our government, but we lack effective means. Elections? Petitions? Protest marches, rallies, demonstrations? We've been there, tried that, and our grievances persist. Amend our Constitution? That's vastly more difficult than winning an election.

To renew our democracy, regular folks in large numbers must voluntarily act together as We the People. Success requires explicit goals and effective strategies, with diverse tactics for attracting allies, educating ourselves, organizing actively, and mobilizing politically. We'll have all of that with our campaign for Citizen Dividends.

The trouble with corporations: Corporations affect every aspect of our lives and our government, yet neither the Declaration nor our Constitution says anything about them.

In America's early decades, state legislatures publicly debated requests for corporate charters, and states only issued charters for corporations that provided a specified public benefit (a bank, for example, or a college). States imposed strict limits on ownership, operations, and duration, and corporations were prohibited from starting or buying other corporations. Charters expired, and were sometimes revoked. We the People were sovereign.

That began to change in the 1820s. As industrial corporations – particularly coal, steel, and railroads – grew larger and wealthier, the owners gained political power. In 1868, a few years after the Civil War, the Fourteenth Amendment was ratified to secure the rights of former slaves. It declared that "All persons born or naturalized in the United States and subject to the jurisdiction thereof, are citizens of the United States and of the State wherein they reside."

Corporations promptly began to cite it in lawsuits, claiming that they were "persons."

One lawsuit, *Santa Clara County v. Southern Pacific Railroad*, reached the Supreme Court in 1886. The Court didn't even deliberate that claim, but simply asserted that corporations ought to be treated as persons, and then applied that assertion to settle other issues in the case. *Corporate personhood* is now generally accepted. Elected representatives never voted to enact it, lawyers and judges simply invented it — a blatant example of "judge-made law." Yet current laws assume, apply, and rely on it.[9]

Corporations are not people. They're artificial entities, created by people. They don't have rights. They only have the privileges we give them through our government.

Corporations are tools, like hammers and computers. Hammers can build homes or smash skulls, and sometimes we accidentally hit our thumbs. Computers spread viruses, hate speech, child pornography, and stolen credit card numbers. Corporations are tools for accumulating wealth. Founders and investors use corporations to limit liability and protect personal assets. When corporations go bankrupt, typically, founders and investors retain their wealth, even while workers lose their jobs and savings.

Some corporations have immense wealth and power; a few have tacit government support, and have been called "too big to fail." Some are experts at extorting money from government, primarily by saying they'll create jobs if they get the money, or that they'll cut or export jobs if they don't. The Supreme Court reaffirmed and extended corporate personhood with its 2010 decision in *Citizens United*. Corporations can now fund political campaigns without disclosure.

We the People have to restrict or reverse corporate personhood — even if that requires us to amend our state constitutions and the U.S. Constitution.

Restricting or reversing corporate personhood, moreover, must include nonprofit corporations. Many nonprofits represent or act as special interests, and many are created to influence elections. The Democratic and Republican parties are nonprofit corporations – each, in fact, is made up of multiple corporations, with specified purposes and coordinated fundraising – and they use their nonprofit status to enhance their power and privileges.

When corporations engage in politics, whether through lobbying, funding campaigns, or running issue ads, they're acting as proxies for their CEOs, directors, and major shareholders — or, with nonprofits, their major donors. In order to assert our sovereignty over corporations, we may have to focus our attention, and our anger, on the individuals who own or run them.

At the same time, however, we want to remember that CEOs and other folks are distinct from their corporate identities. They have spouses, kids, friends, and neighbors, and they dream of a better world for their grandchildren and great-grandchildren. Many CEOs are likely to join the campaign for Citizen Dividends.

The problem with "jobs": The word *jobs*, like *corporations,* is not in the Declaration nor our Constitution. Now it's everywhere in political discourse. Politicians are full of it.

Government got busy with creating jobs in the 1930s, during the Great Depression, when President Franklin Roosevelt's administration declared government to be "the employer of last resort." With the stated goal of putting Americans back to work, the federal government built dams, schools, roads, bridges, and other structures around the country. It even hired artists, actors, writers, musicians, and photographers, and paid them to make art.

Not today. Our modern government is the promoter of the private sector. Instead of creating jobs directly, its stated role is to stimulate economic growth through urging or aiding private companies to create the jobs. That's the rationale for corporate welfare. That's also why tax cuts are often directed toward rich folks and corporations — self-proclaimed "job creators."

When government funds private sector jobs, CEOs and other executives are paid first, and paid well, before any new jobs are created. Job-creating policies inevitably lead to increased inequality.

Every employer knows that hiring is expensive and workers are a recurring cost. Companies constantly seek higher productivity from fewer workers. When companies cut workers, "downsizing," "rightsizing," or "rationalizing production," they're rewarded with higher profits and rising stock prices. Instead of hiring people, therefore, companies employ robots, computers, voice recognition software, and other new technologies. Jobs are disappearing or threatened even for accountants, journalists, lawyers, and doctors, with work performed by software or outsourced to places where professionals are paid less than in the United States.

Normally, moreover, when politicians promise to create jobs, they skip the details. Who gets the jobs? What do the jobs pay? When? Where? Why is government involved? And how, specifically, will taxpayers benefit? Details are vague or lacking because the claims and promises are, mainly, the rhetoric of wishful thinking rooted in ideology. Many politicians are actually promising to fund special interests — they're rewarding or soliciting campaign contributors.

The problem with "jobs" has only one true solution: basic income. Everyone who's unemployed will have boots and bootstraps, money to live on and lift themselves up. We won't expect or depend on government to create jobs for us, neither directly nor indirectly. Creating jobs, therefore, will no longer be government's job.

Regular folks will be spending our basic income dollars, demanding goods and services, stimulating economic activity — thereby creating jobs for ourselves and others. Regular folks will be the job creators.

This will also be good for employers. They'll have more options and flexibility than today, because many folks will prefer to work part-time or variable schedules, perhaps as independent contractors. Business conditions are constantly changing, and employers will be more free to adopt, and adapt to, new technologies and business strategies.

Initial suggestions: For most Americans today, personal liberty is impaired by financial constraints. Many of us cannot afford the time to act as citizens, so our democracy is impaired. Basic economic security is imperative.[*]

- Liberty and the pursuit of happiness: To enhance liberty, happiness, and equality for all Americans, we should ensure that local and state governments can enact their own versions of this plan.
- Democracy and the pursuit of happiness: Our elections and political practices are seriously flawed, so let's use local and state elections to experiment with nonpartisan redistricting,

---

[*] "True individual freedom cannot exist without economic security and independence," Franklin Roosevelt declared in his State of the Union on January 11, 1944. He proposed "a second Bill of Rights under which a new basis of security and prosperity can be established for all."

full disclosure of funding, and other reform initiatives. We'll see what works – when, where, why, and how – and then we can refine those policies and apply them more widely.

- The trouble with corporations: We have to end corporate personhood, at a minimum to ban corporations from participating in politics. Does that require amending state constitutions? Amending the U.S. Constitution? These are huge challenges. We should start immediately.
- The problem with "jobs": Let's tell politicians to stop talking about "jobs," and instead to focus on doing their own jobs. Their jobs are to serve all of us, including future generations, and they can do that by enacting this plan.

Democracy succeeds only when citizens participate actively and consistently. The more engaged we are, in both our numbers and the quality of our engagement, the stronger our democracy. Citizen Dividends will pay us to participate as citizens.

Liberty is never fully secure. Individual citizens must be vigilant, alert for abuses by government and by corporations. We must also be ready to actively resist threats and violations, even when the offenders are our own employers.

This is a plan to liberate all of us — to "secure the blessings of liberty to ourselves and our posterity."

* * * * *

What do you think about our democracy?

How do you feel about your personal liberty?

Liberty and *democracy* are central to our national identity, and Citizen Dividends make these ideals personal. You'll have greater liberty to pursue happiness, with an independent income that's guaranteed and unconditional, unlike a paycheck. You'll also have greater opportunities to demand – and have – an active voice in our government, a stronger democracy.

Are you concerned about government infringing on your liberty? Have you experienced some abuse or violation? Perhaps your taxes were wrongly assessed, or you had an upsetting encounter with federal agents, or your business was harmed by government regulations. Errors, abuses, and excesses happen. When you have a basic income, and our democracy is stronger, you'll be better able to seek redress for any grievances.

Are you concerned about big corporations abusing their privileges? Have you experienced that personally? Perhaps your bank raised the rates on your credit card, or your phone or cable provider charges you for services you don't want, or you sometimes shop at a store that has let hackers steal credit card or Social Security numbers. When we have grievances with corporations, government officials can intervene on our behalf. This plan will make it easier for you to seek and get assistance when you need it.

Are you satisfied with your job? Perhaps your hours were cut, or you were due for a raise but didn't get it. Or your employer refused to give you time off for a family emergency, or altered the terms of your heath care or retirement plan. You might like and respect your boss, but even the best bosses are sometimes wrong. With a secure basic income, you'll have more freedom to look for a better job, if that's what you want. Also more leverage to negotiate with your current boss, or a future boss, about your pay, hours, vacation time, and other conditions.

Do you vote? Do you sometimes donate to causes or candidates? Have you ever volunteered for a political campaign?

If you're like most folks, you vote in major elections, though not midterms, primaries, or runoffs. Perhaps you sometimes email or phone elected officials, go to an occasional rally or meeting, or donate a few dollars. At the same time, though, you probably have reasons for not being more involved. Why bother? Has an election ever produced the changes you desire?

With Citizen Dividends, you'll be getting money from government, not just paying taxes to it. The relationship will be more reciprocal than today. Local and state governments are likely to be more responsive and effective, and our national government smaller and less intrusive.

Does this make sense? Do you think you'll be more active as a citizen? You can start now.

8. To Respect and Protect our Environment

Basic income will bring rapid progress on environmental issues, with sustainable successes.

The obstacles are obvious, clichés, "jobs versus the environment" and "the economy versus the environment." More accurate, though not a cliché, special interests versus the environment. These three phrases distract us from a crucial fact: the real obstacle is us. We demand jobs and depend on economic growth. Special interests promise to provide both, jobs and growth, so we let them despoil and exploit our environment. In this context, *we* represents the conventional consensus, the bipartisan status quo.

Environmental concerns ought to be nonpartisan or transpartisan. When we talk about protecting our environment, many of us use the words *prudent, cautious, restrained,* and *traditional,* synonyms for *conservative. Conservative* is the root of *conservationist,* a synonym for *environmentalist.*[10]

Our environment is *ours,* everyone's. Clean air and clean water are human *needs,* literally, and we rely on government to keep them clean, safe, and healthy. On matters of public safety and public health, anti-government is anti-commonsense and anti-self-interest.

Global warming and climate change: Agents of the status quo – fossil fuel companies primarily, and their allies – deny or distort the evidence of global warming, and tout every doubt, dispute, and disagreement. "I'm not a scientist," politicians proclaim. "No one really knows," as if that excuses their failures to act. But global warming is not waiting.

People are being harmed today. While climate change may not be proven to *cause* specific events, *correlations* are irrefutable. We're seeing more frequent and more destructive floods, droughts, heat waves, mudslides, melting glaciers, coastal erosion, and major storms like hurricanes Sandy and Katrina, typhoon Haiyan, and the Baton Rouge floods. As our planet warms, the climate is becoming unstable, the weather less predictable. Wherever we live, we'll soon be paying higher prices for food, fuel, housing, and insurance.

The prudent response is to act promptly.

A sensible first step is central to this plan: eliminate corporate welfare. Specifically, we'll end subsidies and tax breaks, etc., for producing and consuming fossil fuels. Companies will innovate to become more efficient, developing new products, services, and technologies. The innovations will help American companies prosper in world markets.

Next, the most effective and cost-effective approach – according to economists and environmentalists, liberals and conservatives – is to tax oil, coal, and natural gas: a carbon tax. Fuel prices go up; consumption falls. Some jobs disappear; others are created. People will make their own decisions about what to change, and when and how — and Citizen Dividends will ensure that everyone can afford to make the changes we choose.

Big benefits can come from small taxes, especially if we periodically increase the taxes. Everyone will have escalating incentives to demand efficient cars, homes, appliances, packaging, etc., so businesses will have incentives to supply them. Fuel taxes function as invisible hands, guiding people and companies to do what's best for all of us and future generations.

To maximize market efficacy and efficiency, and to minimize government, we should assess taxes at the mine, well-head, border, or port, wherever the fuel first enters the economic stream. A wholesale tax, in other words, not a retail tax at the gas pump, utility bill, or cash register. Fossil fuel taxes will:

- make fuel prices more predictable.
- reduce pollution of all types, from all sources.
- protect nature and save countless endangered species.
- enhance national security by conserving fossil fuel supplies.
- drive American companies to innovate and become more efficient.
- promote organic farming, through higher costs for synthetic materials.
- reward reuse, redesign, recycling, and other environmentally-positive practices.

All these gains will come through market forces. Our economy depends on fossil fuels, demands them, is addicted to them. Fossil fuel taxes will reduce our dependency and help end our addictions. We'll see real progress — even while rescinding regulations and cutting government programs.

Global warming is global, obviously. Agents of the status quo have said the United States shouldn't act, or can't afford to, until we see progress in China, India, Russia, and elsewhere. Now those countries and almost all others are actively cutting fuel consumption and emissions, prodded partly by the Paris climate agreement. We Americans take pride in being world leaders, and we use far more fossil fuels per capita than people in other countries. Smart fossil fuel taxes will enhance our political, economic, and moral leadership.

Climate concerns compel us to be extra wary of corporations. Consider water. Clean water is a human need; we can't live without it. Corporations are artificial entities and don't have needs. Various industrial activities require water — "fracking," for example, hydraulic fracturing, which pollutes huge quantities of water with toxic chemicals and injects it deep underground. Fossil fuel companies can exist without fracking, and can still profit without it. Using water for profit is different from needing it for survival.

Basic income will free us to focus on real human needs, and free us from the "need" for jobs. We'll be liberated from flawed notions about corporations, and therefore able to regulate them appropriately.

Oil, coal, and natural gas are created by nature, so everyone ought to have a share. *Everyone* includes our grandchildren, their great-grandchildren, and the rest of humanity for generations to come. By taxing fossil fuels and reducing consumption – while providing a basic income for all – we'll promote social justice, economic justice, and environmental justice.*

We also have aesthetic reasons to act. Our Earth is beautiful. Diversity is essential. Species, habitats, and biodiversity are declining or disappearing. Protecting our environment enriches our humanity.

Cities and suburbs: Our environment includes the built environment. Roads, dams, bridges, sewers, and mass transit are public works, built and maintained mostly by government. They're also

---

* *Agrarian Justice* too, as Thomas Paine taught us.

public investments, necessary for local and national prosperity. Yet we often see or read about roads buckling, dams breaking, bridges collapsing, water mains bursting, and oil pipelines leaking and contaminating water supplies. Hundreds of communities, perhaps thousands, have lead in their drinking water.

Urban and suburban neighborhoods are afflicted by crime, poverty, and racial unrest, and pockmarked by vacant lots and empty buildings. Local political campaigns are funded by remote special interests. Major employers, frequently foreign-owned, have immense influence over local officials, local news media, local cultural organizations, and therefore over every resident.

Cities and suburbs will be safer and more prosperous when we have Citizen Dividends. Every resident will have money to spend at local businesses, and that spending will create jobs and generate tax revenues. Local governments will have funds to invest in public safety, public health, education, transit, and so on. Regular folks will have added incentives to act as citizens and demand effective government.

Our federal government sends a lot of money to state and local governments, often with strict mandates about how to spend it — local policies dictated from above. Some of that money is "revenue-sharing." Basic income is revenue-sharing, too, and it eliminates all the middlemen: the bureaucrats, technocrats, lobbyists, and politicians. Regular folks will have greater freedom and power to set policies.

In Flint, Michigan, the lead poisoning was caused by reckless spending cuts and multiple failures by numerous officials. Suppose Flint residents had basic income before that occurred: Their local and state governments would have been better funded and more prudent. If or when lead was detected, residents would have mobilized rapidly to get repairs, remedies, investigations, and maybe prosecutions.

Most cities and suburbs have racial disparities in housing, education, employment, public amenities, and law enforcement. Lawsuits are common. Unrest is a constant concern, with sporadic protests that sometimes explode into riots. Basic income will be a baseline of economic equality — and a starting line toward greater racial, social, and political equality.*

A related issue is gentrification. Wealthier folks move into prime neighborhoods, housing prices go up, and poor residents are squeezed out. The wealthy are white, typically, and they're displacing blacks and Latinos. Instead, current residents can be the gentry, using their basic income to buy the homes they're living in. Neighborhoods will instantly be more stable.

Where the cost of living is high – New York City, Miami, Silicon Valley, counties near Washington D.C., and so on – residents can demand supplements, funded from local revenues. Local businesses might favor supplements to keep their customers from moving away. How much? How to pay for it? Residents will decide.

Urban and suburban residents will clearly benefit from higher fossil fuel taxes, with:

- cleaner air, and therefore lower rates of asthma.
- less traffic congestion, so it's easier to get around.
- walkable neighborhoods, residents less dependent on cars.
- more stable economic conditions for locally-owned businesses.

---

* "We are likely to find that the problems of housing and education, instead of preceding the elimination of poverty, will themselves be affected if poverty is first abolished," Martin Luther King Jr. wrote. "The solution to poverty is to abolish it directly by a now widely discussed measure: the guaranteed income."

- industries with clean technologies, allowing factories to be near homes, parks, and schools.

We can magnify these gains by shifting property taxes off buildings and onto land values. Land is local, limited, and impossible to move or hide, so land value taxes are relatively easy to assess and collect. Buildings deteriorate and depreciate, and each is distinct, so those taxes are complicated; owners often dispute assessments, and can evade or avoid payment, sometimes through fraud or arson.

Where property taxes are 100 percent on the land value, taxes are the same on a luxury building or a vacant lot. Owners of vacant lots have compelling reasons to swiftly build or rebuild. Even a partial tax shift – 80 percent, say, or 60 percent – will promote smart rebuilding of cities, suburbs, and recent sprawl. This is another instance of using taxes as invisible hands to promote public benefits.

When a community invests in schools, parks, mass transit, and such, nearby property values increase. With land value taxes, public investments really are investments; the gains are taxed and money is returned directly and dependably. In most places today, those gains are privatized — captured by wealthy landowners, including speculators. Land value taxes deter speculation. These benefits have been demonstrated in America and around the world. [11]

Urban and suburban neighborhoods will become more distinct and truly local — a welcome change from the sprawl, strip malls, and sameness that characterize countless communities today. Progress will be market-driven, through the self-interest of individuals and businesses. Distinct communities, in turn, are likely to generate new businesses and other innovations, bringing greater prosperity.

Small towns and rural areas: Rural communities and environments are beset with troubles:

- poverty, lack of opportunities, and declining populations.
- conflicts between long-time residents and recent immigrants.
- drug abuse – meth, heroin, oxycontin, etc. – and related crimes.
- air, water, and land polluted by fracking, oil drilling, and coal mining.
- boom and bust cycles; uncontrolled growth followed by abandoned buildings.
- toxic materials transported by trains or trucks that sometimes crash and catch fire, or by pipelines that sometimes leak.

Small town residents will see rapid gains. Even $500 a month will bring a surge of local economic activity and new jobs. Residents will have reasons for hope, and hope is vital for ending the epidemic of abuse and addiction to meth, heroin, and opioids. Local governments will have revenues for public safety and public health, and to invest in public works. Millions of folks will choose to stay, return, or start anew in rural areas, seeking affordable homes, traditional values, and easy access to open spaces and outdoor recreation.

Rural communities will clearly benefit from taxes on takings. Fossil fuel taxes ease the political and economic pressure for drilling, fracking, and mining. Land value taxes can help small towns be more distinct and vibrant. Taxes are based on the rental value of the land, so taxes are an incentive to keep buildings clustered, while protecting farms and preserving land that's fallow, forest, prairie, wetlands, or desert.*

---

* Taxes on takings have many forms. In Bristol Bay, Alaska, in the early 1970s, mayor Jay Hammond, alarmed by a steep increase in Japanese commercial fishing, persuaded residents to tax the taking of salmon. Although that was a burden for local fisherman, who initially opposed the tax, significant revenues came from the Japanese. The whole community gained immensely. Hammond was elected governor in 1974, and was a leader in creating the Alaska Permanent Fund and the Permanent Fund Dividend.

In small towns, far more than big cities, politics and government are obviously personal. Mayors, sheriffs, and councilmembers are neighbors, not just names in the news. Residents see elected officials in grocery stores and at their kids' little league games. When big companies try to steamroll local communities – promising jobs, economic growth, and "development" – casual contacts among residents and officials can help ensure that local values endure.

Rural areas are also home to a category of citizens who've been particularly abused, exploited, and impoverished: Native Americans. Though many tribes have casinos, gambling is a distraction; it's not the solution. Basic income will help all Native Americans, on rural reservations and in urban areas. Plus, this baseline of equality can remind the rest of us about our obligations to respect native rights and sovereignty.*

The gains are sure to grow over time. As rural areas attract new residents, small towns will become increasingly unique, attractive, and prosperous.

Food, farms, and agriculture: Our food system is dominated by agribusiness corporations, and their primary goal is to produce profits. They sow political influence by creating rural jobs and feeding urban folks. And they reap plentiful subsidies, harvesting billions of dollars a year.

Subsidies are almost entirely for major producers of corn, soybeans, wheat, rice, and sorghum. Corn feeds cattle, chickens, and pigs, and produces ethanol and high fructose corn syrup. Soybeans also feed animals, and are processed into protein supplements and

---

* A few tribes distribute casino profits directly, as a basic income. One is the Eastern Band of Cherokee Indians in North Carolina. Appendix 1 has more information about their program.

meat substitutes. Sorghum is mainly animal feed. Those subsidies mean low prices for meat, dairy, eggs, and junk food, thereby promoting unhealthy diets that lead to obesity, diabetes, and heart disease, with higher costs for medical care and health insurance.

Small farms are not subsidized. Vegetables are not subsidized. Organic practices are not subsidized. Yet farmer's markets and organic vegetables are increasingly popular, proof that Americans want – and will pay for – healthier foods.

Agribusinesses use massive amounts of herbicides, pesticides, and synthetic fertilizers. Corn, soybeans, and other crops have been genetically modified to tolerate these chemicals. The chemicals and genetic modifications are safe, the companies tell us, though their claims are mostly based on research they funded. Independent scientists disagree.[12]

Public policies should foster agriculture, not agribusiness. Culture cultivates complex, resilient relationships between and among people, communities, and nature. Business seeks short-term gains and profits. Agriculture respects nature and protects the land. Agribusiness is business first.

Some farm subsidies are corporate welfare, and should be rather easy to cut. Others help farmers keep farming, and we'll redesign those. Reforms are imperative, even urgent, because farmers are already coping with a warming planet and changing climate, with a significant increase in floods, droughts, fungal infections, insect infestations, and price fluctuations. Protecting farms and farmers has to be a national priority.

Farmers will profit from smart tax reforms. Land value taxes help protect and preserve farmland. Rates are low on land that's farmed or fallow, but higher on land with buildings, so developers have incentives to cluster buildings in towns and city centers. Fossil fuel taxes will encourage farmers to shift away from synthetic chemicals, and toward more traditional, sustainable, and organic practices. Farmers, not government regulators, will drive the changes. Small farms will benefit the most, because big agribusinesses are more entrenched. Compared with today, small farms and family farms will be more likely to prosper.

Agriculture reforms are also a way to slow the rate of global warming. Farmers can remove carbon from the air and sequester it in the soil through organic methods, integrated pest management, integrated livestock operations, and permaculture. These practices are similar to, and based on, natural processes over millions of years.

Our Earth and our future: Humans have severely altered our planet over the past century, more than we know. Modern industries – fossil fuels, plastics, chemicals, agribusiness, aviation, automobiles, pharmaceuticals, electronics, and nuclear power – generate huge amounts of waste, much of it toxic. Our air, water, and food are contaminated. Our bodies are contaminated, even newborns.

Corporations synthesize and manufacture materials for their purposes, seeking profits. Testing is limited, conducted mainly by private corporations. Each new compound can affect the action of myriad others that are already being used. Chemical actions and interactions vary among species and with changing weather and climate. Long-term and cumulative impacts are unknowable.

Genetically-modified foods were introduced in the 1990s, though not because consumers wanted GMOs. The demand came from agribusiness, a demand for higher profits. Monsanto manufactured Roundup (glyphosate), a weed-killer, and then engineered plant genes to make the crops glyphosate-resistant, Roundup-Ready.

Glyphosate is made in China, and millions of tons are used every year in the United States. Independent research indicates that glyphosate may cause cancer, birth defects, miscarriages, infertility, and related problems. Some GMOs also appear to cause or correlate with health problems. Modified genes are now spreading to the weeds, so agribusiness corporations are developing another generation of GMO crops and herbicides.[13]

During the Deepwater Horizon oil drilling disaster of 2010, BP used 1.9 million gallons of oil dispersant Corexit to clean up the mess. That was intended to reduce the damage, although it may have only reduced the immediate disgust, anger, and blame. The Gulf of Mexico is an extremely valuable and vital fishing area. Yet BP used Corexit in an untested procedure, injecting it at a depth of 5,000 feet. Scientists now have evidence that Corexit is toxic to marine life, and that mixing it with oil increases the toxicity.[14]

Plastic trash in our oceans totals more than 260,000 tons, more than 5 trillion pieces. A lot of it travels on the ocean's surface, collected by currents in conspicuous clumps. A lot more is on the ocean floor, or drifting through the depths, or deposited on beaches around the world. Countless bits are invisible or nearly so, including plastic microbeads from cosmetics. Some gets eaten by fish and other creatures, including those that humans then eat. Plastic trash also befouls streams, rivers, roadsides, deserts, and forests. Landfills are overflowing. Plastic is forever.[15]

Glyphosate, GMOs, synthetic chemicals, and plastic trash are products of current policies and ideologies. Special interests versus the environment, and the special interests are winning.

Our Earth is endangered. Numerous species are going extinct. We humans could go too, possibly with a sudden population crash.

Protecting our environment is protecting ourselves. Respecting nature is self-respect.

Initial suggestions: With Citizen Dividends, we'll be less anxious about higher taxes and prices, and more prepared to assert our sovereignty over the special interests that are plundering our planet.

- Global warming and climate change: This plan doesn't require us to accept the science, only to pursue our self-interests. The most reliable and conservative path forward is to gradually and periodically increase fossil fuel taxes. To promote markets and private enterprise, we should assess taxes at the source, where fuels first enter the economic stream.

- Cities and suburbs: We want and can readily have more attractive walkable cities, so let's shift property taxes off buildings and onto land. Perhaps we should also cut sales taxes, business taxes, and such, to make land value taxes the main or sole source of funds for local governments.

- Small towns and rural areas: Let's be sure rural folks have a meaningful voice in the decisions that affect them. Residents will especially benefit from taxes on fossil fuels, to minimize damage from mining, drilling, fracking, and associated activities. We should tax all takings (minerals, timber, land values, etc.) and ensure that at least some of the revenues stay local.

- Food, farms, and agriculture: Before agribusiness grew so powerful, farming was very different from today. There were few vast fields with a single crop, and no factory mass production of meat or poultry. We should restore and renew traditional practices, with policies that favor small farms, fresh vegetables, organic methods, and local agriculture. A first step is to cut the subsidies to big agribusiness companies.

• Our Earth and our future: Our Earth is unique and sacred, and we have a duty to be good stewards. We should apply the *precautionary principle*: when in doubt, be cautious, prevent harm. Demand independent testing of synthetic materials – herbicides, pesticides, fertilizers, and GMOs – plus proper labels.

These policies are prudent, cautious, restrained, traditionalist, and conservative, though also urgent. Every delay compounds the environmental harms and costs.

Protecting our environment, truly, means protecting it from us. As individuals and as a species, we must reduce our impacts. Beyond that: we can, should, and perhaps must actively seek to reverse the damage, the massive harms we've inflicted over the past century. Folks might choose careers in science, call for policies that promote restorative and regenerative practices, and perhaps contribute a portion of our Citizen Dividends to these causes.

Our environment. This plan, by including everyone, can ensure that progress is sustainable.

*   *   *   *   *

What do you think about our environment?

Are you concerned or angry about global warming? About lead in the drinking water? About species extinction and the loss of biodiversity?

Most of us live in cities or suburbs. We encounter nature primarily via lawns, parks, and gardens. Our food comes from restaurants and supermarkets. Waste and trash are picked up and carried away, or flushed away — *away*, wherever that is.

Imagine that you have an extra $500 a month, perhaps $1,000 a month, added to what you earn. Also suppose fuel prices are higher than today — and predictable, rising gradually through small, periodic tax increases. That means escalating prices for gasoline, plastics, electricity, synthetic chemicals, and manufactured goods. Higher shipping costs, too, for stuff that's made or grown in China and other remote locations.

Your decisions about what, when, and how to change – or not change – will truly be yours. If you view global warming as a serious threat, you'll breathe easier, knowing that we're making real progress. If you believe it's a hoax or exaggerated, well, you can consume as you choose, with less blaming and shaming than today. The political climate will be relatively calm, and that's something all of us ought to welcome.

Do you commute? Are you sometimes – or often, even daily – upset by traffic jams, transit breakdowns, and other troubles? With basic income, you and your neighbors may be more inclined to invest in public works and infrastructure. After all, if we don't invest for the future, we're actually choosing inadequate services, lower quality of life, and higher long-term costs. Your city or town is likely to be more livable and beautiful.

Do you know anyone who was harmed by the Baton Rouge floods in 2016? What about Hurricane Sandy in 2012 or Hurricane Katrina in 2005? A relative, perhaps, or friend-of-a-friend? In floods, hurricanes, and earthquakes, poor folks are usually harmed the most. Some can't afford to prepare or flee, and many don't have adequate insurance. You might consider these inequities when the next event occurs. Basic income will help all residents recover more readily. This plan will save lives.

Are you worried that pesticides, herbicides, or GMO foods might cause long-term harms to you, your kids, or your grandkids? With higher fossil fuel taxes, fast food and junk food will cost more than today, while local organic foods are more available. You might make it a priority to prepare healthy meals with your family. Perhaps you'll plant a garden and grow some of your own food.

Have you sometimes smelled oil or chemicals in the air or your tap water? You and your neighbors will have greater power to press elected officials to be vigilant — ideally to prevent leaks, spills, and accidents, though also to respond rapidly if something happens. One way to prevent problems is to enact stronger laws so we can prosecute CEOs and revoke corporate charters.

Do you enjoy hiking, hunting, fishing, or bird watching? Vacations at the beach? In recent decades, these activities have become less accessible and less appealing. If we don't act soon, you might someday talk about outdoor recreation, and your grandchildren will think you're making it up — just telling stories.

9. To Nurture Peace and Security for All

We pray for peace, often, in sacred and secular settings. Basic income may be the answer to our prayers, a true path toward world peace.

Today, "world peace" and "pray for peace" are platitudes. Conventional policies and practices perpetuate conflicts, sometimes provoke conflicts. Underlying resentments persist, undermining our hopes, prayers, and good intentions.

Peace can be the centerpiece in America's foreign policy, the primary goal or organizing principle. When We the People demand it, it will be.

Secure borders: America's borders are not secure — not from terrorists, immigrants crossing illegally, heroin or cocaine or other drugs, or infectious diseases like Zika or Ebola. The border with Mexico may be impossible to fully secure, too teeming with commerce, tourists, and residents who have business on both sides. Airport security is a problem and hassle throughout the country.

Our virtual borders are also vulnerable, and under constant surveillance that sometimes fails. Cyberterrorists can attack from anywhere in the world, and some are trained by, or working for, hostile governments. Cyberterrorists steal credit card and Social Security numbers, empty bank accounts, and encrypt computer files and hold them for ransom paid in untraceable bitcoin. Individuals, businesses, and government agencies – including the U.S. military and our electoral systems – are targets.

Terrorists troll social media, seeking people who are alienated or dejected, offering solace and a cause to believe in, enticing and exhorting folks to attack Americans. Also online are instructions for improvised explosives that anyone can build with available materials. When terrorists are willing or want to die, they're nearly unstoppable; one or two can cause multiple deaths and mass destruction.

This plan empowers us in two ways, as citizens and with dividends; both are necessary. Consider warnings to be vigilant for unattended bags, backpacks, and such; "If you see something, say something." Most of us discount or disregard the warnings, partly because we're worrying about how to pay our bills. Instead, everyone will have economic security and monthly reminders that we're stakeholders, with a personal commitment to public safety. Vigilant folks are vital for preventing mass shootings, terrorist attacks, and other crimes — and this plan may be our best or only hope for greater security.

We'll also be safer if there's a pandemic flu or anything like Zika or Ebola; public health experts say "when, not if." Today, when we have a cold or flu, most of us go to work; we have no choice, we need the money. Our co-workers, customers, clients, etc., also have to work, so we're often around folks who are coughing or sneezing. When everyone can afford to stay home, many of us will stay healthier. In any pandemic, basic income will save countless lives.

Immigration reform: Immigrants are "taking our jobs," people say, and many of us are anxious or angry. The jobs they're taking, however, are mainly low pay, low skill, hard labor, or uncertain hours

— jobs Americans don't want and won't take. Other jobs offer good wages and salaries, in the computer industry for instance, but companies earn higher profits with immigrants and H-1B visas. Citizen Dividends are for citizens only. We'll be less anxious about our jobs, probably less angry, and therefore more likely to keep calm as we consider reform options.

Immigrants obey the law and pay taxes, and many pay into Social Security they'll never collect. They start businesses, serve in the military, go to school, and educate their kids to work hard and be responsible. Nearly all Americans are descended from immigrants. When citizens have basic economic security, guaranteed, we'll likely be more welcoming and willing to respect immigrants' contributions to our society.

Immigration issues also involve core American values about love, loyalty, and family. Current policies divide families, sometimes tear them apart. Sensible reforms will reaffirm our commitment to family values.

Family concerns were clearly evident in 2014, when 68,000 unaccompanied children arrived from Honduras, Guatemala, and El Salvador after travelling north through Mexico. These were kids seeking to reunite with parents in the United States, or kids sent by parents or grandparents who feared for their kids' safety in their home countries. Countless kids died on the journey, or were robbed or raped. That influx was incited by problems in their home countries, a rising incidence of gangs, violence, illegal drugs, and social breakdown. These problems persist. Unaccompanied kids cross the border every day, or try and perhaps don't make it.

We could offer to help Hondurans, etc., implement versions of basic income. Our government already gives those countries financial assistance, so we'd mainly be asking them to redirect those dollars. Residents will have money for food, clothes, and shelter, the means to live with dignity and to demand effective government. Residents will stay home. Folks in the U.S. illegally will have reasons to go home.*

Hondurans, etc., will be stronger allies in stopping illegal drugs and eliminating terrorism — especially if we help them in this way.

With basic income as a first step toward immigration reform, everyone wins: regular folks, small businesses, big companies, local communities, and our country as a whole.

Pursuing peace: To make peace the centerpiece in American policy, we have to resolve four interrelated obstacles:
- Millions of us have jobs that depend on military spending.
- Wars, and preparing for wars, are money-making opportunities.
- Military contractors spend huge sums on lobbying and campaign contributions.
- Politicians are afraid of being portrayed as weak, soft, or indecisive on terrorism and national security.

When we have Citizen Dividends, regular folks won't be so constrained by our jobs, and politicians won't be so controlled by special interests. Everyone, including folks who work for military contractors, even the CEOs, will be freer to focus on peace — and to demand it.

A crucial step is to cut the waste and excess from military spending. Contractors and their allies will try to stop the cuts, of

---

* This is more than conjecture; it's already happening. Mexicans are going home voluntarily. Over recent years, there's been a net outflow from the United States, and that's partly because Mexico already gives money directly to the poor through conditional cash transfers. The benefits are well-documented. Brazil, Columbia, Peru, and other countries also have conditional programs with proven benefits.

course, deploying their usual two-pronged tactics: jobs on one side, fear on the other. The jobs card will no longer be a trump, so they'll double-down on fear: Fear of Russia and China. Fear of terrorism, Islamic fundamentalism, and other ill-defined abstractions. Fear of nuclear weapons in North Korea, Pakistan, and Iran, and further proliferation. Fear that terrorists will get hold of a nuclear bomb, or nuclear material for a dirty bomb, or chemical or biological weapons. Fear of cyberwarfare.

The fears are often overstated or misdirected. Russia's economy is a mess, the government is blatantly corrupt, extreme poverty is increasing, and wealthy Russians are buying homes in New York and London; military decline is inevitable. China has billions of reasons to maintain peace with us. Their economy depends on trade with the United States, and the same big corporations operate in both countries. More than 300,000 Chinese, sons and daughters of the elite, attend American colleges and universities.

On terrorism, Islamic fundamentalism, nuclear weapons, dirty bombs, proliferation, and cyberwarfare: our security depends on "soft power," diplomacy. Our best, often only, options are to work with allies to impose sanctions, freeze foreign assets, and stop the transfer of weapons and materials. Of course we must be prepared to deploy our military, on our own if necessary, yet we also have to acknowledge the limits of military force. Every U.S. airstrike, even when properly targeted and perfectly executed, is a recruiting event for terrorists.

As we cut the waste and excess, we also have to reassess. How many F-35s are we building, and why? What is the current mission of the B-2 bomber? Should we build another aircraft carrier or next-generation nuclear weapons? Those programs reflect a 20th century Cold War mindset, and may be ineffective in 21st century conflicts. Cyberwars can't be won with cruise missiles.

We'll be safer. Military leaders and policymakers won't be so distracted by efforts to create jobs, nor so burdened by bloated bureaucracies. The U.S. military will still be, by far, the world's largest and most powerful.

We'll be more prosperous. With the money we save, we can cut taxes, reduce the deficit, invest in infrastructure, or increase our Citizen Dividends. America's economy will be stronger.

We'll be more united. If any country threatens us – funding terrorists, say, or mobilizing troops – we'll likely have the political will and diplomatic leverage to impose effective sanctions. Even if it's Iran or Saudi Arabia, and sanctions cause fuel prices to rise. Even if it's Russia or China.

America will also have greater power to persuade or pressure other countries to scale back their militaries and to stop selling weapons. The leading exporters are America, France, Russia, China, Sweden, Italy, and Germany, and about half of all exports are American. The stated reasons are to defeat terrorists, support allies, and deter wars. In all these countries, however, particularly ours, politicians are most concerned with domestic matters, creating jobs and promoting economic growth. Furthermore, countries don't simply "sell weapons." Governments subsidize military contractors, contractors lobby or bribe politicians, and countries actively compete for customers. Exports are evidence that jobs, profits, and economic growth are more important than peace. We have to shift our priorities.[16]

In effect, through who we elect, every American will have a choice: A bigger military, with more F-35s, etc., or more money in our hands? Export weapons or nurture peace?

People around the world will be asking similar questions. Do I want a basic income? Can my country maintain peace with a smaller military? How can we encourage nearby countries to cut their militaries?

Ending war and terrorism: Effective government is a prerequisite. When governments falter or fail, even briefly, terrorists and militants can arise or infiltrate, and cause governments to fail faster. Wherever militants gain control and hold territory, they impose order. Residents tend to accept the militant regime, even welcome it, tolerating tyranny or theocracy rather than enduring the chaos of war. That's how the Taliban reclaimed large parts of Afghanistan.

Where there is war or terrorism today, American policy is to identify a presumably responsible entity – typically the government, sometimes an anti-government faction – and provide support. First send money, sometimes loads of cash. Then send food, tents, clothes, and medicine. Then small arms, while training and advising local forces. Then, if fighting crosses an undefined line, drones, airstrikes, and U.S. special forces. Worst-case scenario: "boots on the ground."

ISIS, the Taliban, Boko Haram, al-Qaeda, al-Nusra, al-Shabaab, et al., pay their soldiers, and those paychecks are recruiting tools. Basic income will recruit people for peace. Residents of those regions will have concrete incentives to end wars and prevent terrorism, even if the distribution is delayed by fighting, factions, or other factors. Our government can provide funds. We'll save billions of dollars in every conflict, while also saving countless lives. Americans will be safer, especially U.S. troops and diplomats.

Three factors – the "resource curse," extreme nationalism, and militant Islam – characterize current and recent wars. Basic income is a remedy for all three.

Resource curse is the term social scientists use to describe a tragic yet well-known fact: countries with plentiful natural wealth – oil, gold, diamonds, and so on – are often afflicted by war, terrorism, autocratic rulers, or environmental devastation; all of these, in many cases. Rulers or factions plunder nature, and use the money to increase their wealth and power. We see this in Russia, Iraq, Iran, Libya, Syria, Nigeria, Saudi Arabia, Turkmenistan, Congo, and other countries, too many others; diverse circumstances, though the same pathology.

An alternative is Alaska, which has the Permanent Fund Dividend. And Norway, where oil revenues fund universal social programs, including free education and free medical care. Natural wealth should be a blessing — and it will be when countries tax what people take from nature, and use that money to fund dividends for everyone. For resource-cursed countries, this is an escape plan.

Extreme nationalism is very different from the healthy form. Extremists exploit patriotism, wielding it as a weapon to silence critics, attack opponents, and aggrandize themselves. Where extremists hold power, they sometimes start wars to divert attention from domestic troubles — for example, Vladimir Putin and Russia's incursions into Ukraine.

Healthy nationalism was when Ukrainians overthrew a corrupt regime in the nonviolent Orange Revolution of 2004, and again in the Euromaidan protests of early 2014. Then, however, extremism spread through the east, increasing social, political, and economic unrest. Russia cited that unrest, after inciting it, then annexed Crimea and sent in troops, launching a war along the border. Suppose Ukrainians enact a basic income. They'll all have reasons to reunite the country and to demand peace. Individuals, families, and communities will be free, ideally, to choose the best from east and west.

Militant Islam is the ideology of ISIS, al-Qaeda, et al., groups that have declared war on America and the West. Their tactics include suicide bombings, mass murders, mass kidnappings, raping and selling women as sex slaves, beheading or burning people alive. Asymmetric warfare, low-cost yet terribly effective, weapons and tactics that we cannot defeat with drones, airstrikes, or cruise missiles.

The real danger, though, is not Islam, not fundamentalist Islam, not even "radical Islamic terrorism." The real danger is militancy, the use of violence to impose an ideology or way of living. That's coercion, not religion. True faith cannot be coerced. Coercion defiles religion. Militant Islamists use religion as a pretext, smokescreen, or weapon while they rape, abuse, exploit, plunder, and murder. An answer to militarism, and an antidote, is true religion. True Islam is a religion of peace.

Two or three factors typically combine. Iraq was cursed by oil when the country was founded after World War I, and cursed by extreme nationalism under both Saddam Hussein and the Shia-led government that followed. ISIS is all three: extreme nationalist militant Sunnis funded by oil revenues.

Imagine Iraq if basic income had been introduced soon after Saddam Hussein was ousted in April, 2003. Dividends from oil revenues would have united Shias, Sunnis, and Kurds. Every Iraqi would have had money to rebuild their homes, businesses, and communities, plus real incentives to create stable representative government, local and national. Oil revenues would have funded the rebuilding of the country. Saving thousands of American lives, saving trillions of U.S. taxpayer dollars, saving many hundred thousands of Iraqi lives.*

This approach would have prevented the rise of ISIS and precluded countless incidents of terrorism in America and around the world. We would almost certainly have seen democracy spread rapidly throughout the region and beyond.

Peace and security for all: In troubled regions or countries, only one force has the power to attain enduring peace: local residents.

Wherever there's war or terrorism, a huge majority of residents are civilians. Also a huge majority of victims. Civilians are the wives, kids, parents, and neighbors of the tiny fraction of the population who are or become soldiers, militants, or terrorists. Even just the promise of basic income will give every resident concrete incentives to locate, arrest, and prosecute suspected terrorists and militants.

We can support and encourage people, or pressure them, by redirecting U.S. foreign aid, particularly military aid. Maybe put aid money in escrow until after a country acts. Maybe make basic income an agenda item for trade negotiations, possibly a precondition. Maybe rescind trade agreements, such as preferred status, until countries implement their programs.

America can lead, other countries will follow. If we delay, they'll go ahead of us. Who might be first?

Namibia? Namibians know about basic income, thanks to a privately-funded pilot project that ran from late 2007 through 2009. A majority want it nationwide, and government officials have said they

---

* This almost happened. In the summer of 2003, Senators Lisa Murkowski, Republican from Alaska, and Mary Landrieu, Democrat from Louisiana, introduced a resolution calling for an "Iraqi Freedom Fund," modeled on Alaska's Permanent Fund Dividend. Secretary of State Colin Powell testified in Congress and expressed his support. The debate about Iraq is in Appendix 3.

support that. But Namibia is a poor country and any version would require outside funding.*

Brazil? Under a law that passed the Senate unanimously in 2004, every Brazilian has a right to a minimum income. The Bolsa Familia provides conditional cash transfers to the poor, and in 2016 the program helped more than 60 million people, 30 percent of the population of 200 million. They might expand it to create a full basic income.

Tunisia? The Arab Spring began there in 2011, after a fruit vendor's suicide sparked the Jasmine Revolution. Tunisians elected a transitional government and ratified a secular constitution. In 2014, they held successful elections for a parliament and a new president. The 2015 Nobel Peace Prize was awarded to the National Dialogue Quartet, a coalition of labor, business, legal, and human rights groups. But the Prize is not a guarantee, and ISIS terrorists are active. Tunisians might lead again, with a version of basic income. Other countries might follow again, Algeria, Libya, Egypt, Bahrain, and so on, this time with lasting successes.

The country that acts first will be especially honored, with a unique place in world history.

- Perhaps Greece, to end the austerity policies that crippled their economy.
- Or Cuba, to secure their egalitarian values as they open to American trade and tourists.
- Or South Africa, where labor unions and religious groups already endorse Basic Income Grants.
- Or East Timor, a poor Pacific Island nation that may want to lead toward real progress on global warming.

---

* The pilot project was in Otjivero-Omitara, a rural village, and 930 people got unconditional monthly payments of N$100, equal to about U.S.$12. That small amount produced big benefits, with significant progress on health, education, social equality, and entrepreneurship. More information is in Appendix 3.

- Or Nigeria, which has oil wealth, but struggles with extreme poverty, environmental devastation, and Boko Haram militants.

Canada, Finland, Holland, and Italy are planning or conducting pilot projects, and one of them might be first. Elected officials have endorsed the idea in Ireland, Scotland, France, Germany, and India. Public campaigns are underway in South Korea, Australia, and New Zealand.

When any country enacts any version, their neighbors will know — and might be motivated to follow, possibly to overthrow a bad government. Basic income in Namibia could help liberate Congo, Angola, and Zimbabwe. Ukrainians might spread the idea to Belarus and Russia. A program in Jordan, Turkey, Iraq, or Lebanon may be the key to peace in Syria — an indirect strategy to end that tragedy, though perhaps the fastest way to expel ISIS, oust Bashar al-Assad, and entice Syrian refugees to return home and rebuild their country.

We could soon see peace in the Middle East. In Israel, income inequality is increasing, and basic income will promote prosperity, political unity, and national security. A Palestinian program might be funded by Arab countries, and will likely lead to a responsible government that can halt terrorist attacks and speed the transition to a peaceful Palestinian state. Israelis and Palestinians, regular folks and their governments, will have a firm foundation for negotiations. Enduring peace is achievable, perhaps fairly soon.

In time, maybe within just a few years, many nations will have their own variations.

Initial suggestions: We're dreaming, imagining, and fantasizing, boldly and unashamedly. This is how new ideas emerge. Dreams and fantasies come first, playful conjecture, followed by public discussions and thoughtful debates that lead to explicit plans. Then, ideally, come action and success and a better world.

- Secure borders: America is vulnerable, so let's act promptly, compromising where necessary. We'll be more united and more vigilant, with more secure borders, seaports, airports, public spaces, and virtual borders.

- Immigration reform: With Citizen Dividends for citizens only, we'll end the political impasse, and then we can calmly consider our options. We should also offer to help Honduras, Guatemala, El Salvador, and Mexico implement their own versions.

- Pursuing peace: Let's get serious about eliminating waste and excess from military spending, while we also reassess and redesign the U.S. military for the 21st century. We should vigorously press other countries to cut their military spending and stop exporting weapons, while we end our exports. The more we cut, the more leverage we'll have to press other countries; the more they cut, the safer we'll be — a virtuous spiral.

- Ending war and terrorism: Where war or terrorism is occurring or seems imminent, our first response should be to promote or provide a basic income for residents of the region. Offer funds. Offer administrative support. Put money in escrow if fighting prevents distribution or a government opposes it.

- Peace and security for all: Let's tell the world that this is what America stands for — Economic security for people everywhere. Personal dignity for people everywhere. Peace everywhere. Tell the world, and act to make it so.

Some countries will include people at age 12 or 15, others at 18 or 21. The basic income might be $20 a month in Afghanistan, South Sudan, Yemen, Haiti, and other extremely poor places. Perhaps $30 or $50 in Honduras, Guatemala, and El Salvador. Perhaps $60 or $100 in countries with oil wealth, like Iraq, Libya, and Nigeria, though probably starting smaller and then increasing the amount as they escape the resource curse and implement overdue reforms.

When America helps any country get started, our support will truly be an investment, unlike current foreign aid. Those countries will be on track to become self-sufficient.

We'll save a huge amount of money. Every bomb, drone, or cruise missile costs tens or hundreds of thousands of dollars. Every hour of flight time in an F-16, F-35, etc., costs tens of thousands of dollars, even testing and training flights. Wars are horribly expensive. Peace is happily economical.

This pro-peace strategy will also bring rapid progress on global warming and climate change. The U.S. military consumes huge quantities of fossil fuels, mainly in routine operations, training troops, building weapons, and transporting troops and equipment. War increases fuel consumption immensely, along with fuel waste: oil burned or spilled in attacks on wells, pipelines, refineries, terminals, tankers, and trucks. Oil facilities are sometimes set on fire deliberately to delay or distract enemy troops, and to deprive people, companies, and governments of revenue. War also destroys huge quantities of steel, copper, rare earth elements, and other natural materials.

Every war, regardless of who, when, where, why, or how, is a war against our planet. Every war, therefore – no matter where or how it's fought, no matter the apparent outcome, and no matter where we live – harms our children and grandchildren and great-grandchildren.

Americans can lead the world toward enduring peace.

*   *   *   *   *

Do you dream about, or pray for, world peace? Do you think we can achieve it?

Are you concerned about border security to stop drugs, immigrants, and terrorists?

What would you have America do about the fighting in Iraq, Afghanistan, Syria, Yemen, or Ukraine?

Imagine that you, your spouse, your friends, your neighbors, and every adult American has a basic income – $500 a month, perhaps, or $1,000 – added to what you earn. Consider how this might affect your feelings and ideas about these issues. Also consider our country as a whole, our sense of unity and patriotism, our national identity.

Recall a time when you were told to be alert for suspicious people or packages. "If you see something, say something." Did you look around? Did you feel anxious? Did you feel reassured? When economic security is guaranteed, and everyone has a stronger sense of citizenship, more folks are likely to act and all of us will be safer.

Are you concerned about Zika, a pandemic flu, or other diseases? During the Ebola outbreak in 2014, did you worry when someone sneezed or coughed? Most of us sometimes go to work when we're ill; we have no choice, we need the money. With a basic income, you'll be able to stay home; other folks, too. You and your family will be healthier.

Are you anxious about immigrants and jobs? Is your job secure? Only citizens get Citizen Dividends. You'll have more options for your job, your family, and your future.

Consider immigrants you know, maybe your parents or grandparents, maybe your neighbors, classmates, or co-workers. They came to America seeking better lives, pursuing happiness. Right? Are they citizens? Eligible to become citizens? Every immigrant, including the undocumented, will have added incentives to work hard, pay taxes, obey the law, and seek citizenship. Should we offer citizenship? What do you think?

When you hear people speaking Spanish, do you sometimes wonder where they're from? Do you ever ask why they left? If their home country had a version of this plan, do you suppose they might have stayed home? Would you support using American aid to help other countries get started?

Have you been to Iraq or Afghanistan, perhaps while serving in the U.S. military? How do you feel about the situation today, and about ISIS proliferating to Syria, Libya, and beyond? Are you sad? Frustrated? Furious?

Have you visited any country that's suffered a recent terrorist attack — France, Belgium, India, or Nigeria? Have you been to Israel?

Recall a few highlights from your trip, particular people, places, or experiences. If you've never been outside the United States, select a country you might like to visit. Now imagine that country with a version of basic income. Consider what this might mean and do for the people there. Would you like them to have these opportunities?

If you believe these ideas make sense, you might join the movement to make this happen. You can help save countless lives.

10. We the People Renewed

With the Declaration of Independence, the Founders asserted our rights and reasons to govern ourselves. With our Constitution, they designed, ordained, and established our national government. With the Bill of Rights, they affirmed the rights of individual citizens and placed explicit limits on our national government.

We'll reaffirm the Founders' ideals and values, and make them our own, with Citizen Dividends. Each of us and all of us, as equals, will have the means to assert our rights, participate as citizens, and act together as We the People.

We the People of the United States, in order to form a more perfect union: When the Founders convened in Philadelphia in 1787, there were armed rebellions within states, conflicts between states, and foreign threats to the newborn nation. The national government was a confederation, with no power to resolve these challenges. It was too small, too poor, too weak.

Now it's too big, too powerful, too beholden to special interests, and too broken to serve common interests.

Our union will be more perfect. Every American will have a real sense of reciprocity with our national government — reasons and resources to make it the right size, with the right powers only, and then to keep it right.

We also have to transform our political practices. Initial suggestions:

- Real people only: A core principle is one person, one vote. When corporations participate in politics, CEOs and owners use company money to multiply their influence; in effect, they have two votes, or hundreds or thousands of votes. We must get corporations out of politics.

- Local focus: Electoral districts should be compact and contiguous, uniting neighbors and neighborhoods, ideally spanning local, state, and federal jurisdictions. Gerrymandering, regardless of how or why, is antidemocratic.[17]

- Full disclosure: We have a right, and a responsibility, to know who's funding causes, parties, and candidates. Today, a huge amount of money comes from the superrich, and donors can conceal their identities. Full disclosure is vital for restoring trust in our political system.[18]

- Citizen-funded campaigns: Political funding can be fair, open, and truly democratic – while protecting everyone's rights to free speech – through a voucher system. Every American might get vouchers for $20, $50, or $100 a year, an amount set at each level, local, state, and federal. Candidates and parties will be funded by regular folks; they'll seek our vouchers and our votes.[19]

- Voting reform: Elections can be more meaningful and more democratic – also less divisive, less negative, and less expensive – with Ranked Choice Voting. Voters indicate a

1st choice, 2nd choice, and 3rd choice. The 1st choices are counted. If no one has more than 50 percent, the candidate with the fewest votes is eliminated, and those voters have their 2nd choices counted; the process repeats until someone surpasses 50 percent. Winners have majority support and real mandates to govern. RCV is also a strong incentive to run positive issue-focused campaigns, because every candidate will want to be voters' second or third choice at least.[20]

- Pragmatic primaries: One option is to have all candidates on a single ballot, an "open," "blanket," or "jungle" primary, then advance the top four to the general election and use RCV. California, Louisiana, and other states have open primaries, but advance the top two, even when they're from the same party. The top four are likely to include both major parties and often "third" party or independent candidates.[21]

- Truly impartial procedures: The Federal Election Commission is deadlocked and dysfunctional by design. The six members are three Democrats and three Republicans, and any action requires a majority. The FEC could have seven members: two Democrats, two Republicans, and three who are truly independent or members of "third" parties.[22]

More possibilities: weekend voting, mandatory voting, or making election day a holiday; automatic universal voter registration; affirming the right to vote by adding it to our Constitution; proportional representation with multi-member districts; eliminating the electoral college or bypassing it with the National Popular Vote, a compact that several states have already endorsed.[23]

Let's experiment in our state and local governments, the "laboratories of democracy." We'll see what works and what doesn't, and where and how and why. Then we can adapt and improve the best practices, applying them where we live and for our national elections. We the People want and deserve – and can have – a more perfect union.

Establish justice: The Founders sought justice, and fought and sacrificed to achieve it, yet many of them owned slaves. Ending slavery required the Civil War and the 13th, 14th, and 15th Amendments. Another original injustice persisted until 1920, when, after decades of organizing, protesting, and struggling, women won the right to vote via the 19th Amendment.

This history conveys valuable lessons. The Founders were wealthy white men. Their doubts and disputes regarding slavery are documented, yet self-interest prevailed. They didn't even question the status quo regarding women. Women also accepted it; at the Seneca Falls convention in 1848, only a minority of female attendees signed the Declaration of Sentiments. One lesson: we default to the familiar, normally. When ideas are unproved, risky, or radical, most of us refuse to act, leaving the status quo intact.

A second lesson is that justice requires government. Partly because we default to the familiar, and partly because we pursue perceived self-interests, we often overlook other people's needs, rights, and concerns. The voiceless and powerless are left on the sidelines. Government – good government, with equal access, honorable courts, and functioning legislatures – is necessary. Everyone must have equal and effective opportunities to participate.

And a third lesson: justice requires time and effort. Individuals have to commit and work together, often in large groups, sometimes over decades or centuries.

Blacks and women live with continuing inequities and discrimination. So do Native Americans, Latinos, and Asians. And Muslims and atheists. And folks who are gay, lesbian, and transgender. And immigrants, documented and undocumented. And poor folks of all backgrounds and identities.

We have work to do – meaningful, sacred work – to truly establish justice.

Insure domestic tranquility: The American Revolution victory did not bring tranquility. Veterans were unpaid, wounded, disabled, and impoverished, and many petitioned for redress of their grievances. In Massachusetts and other states, veterans mounted armed rebellions.

Domestic tranquility is not ensured today, not even close. Our tranquility can be disrupted at any moment by a mass shooting or terrorist attack. The list is long and growing: Oklahoma City, Columbine, 9/11, Virginia Tech, Fort Hood, Tucson, Aurora, Newtown, Boston, the Washington Navy Yard, Isla Vista, Charleston, Oregon, San Bernardino, Orlando, Dallas — we're becoming numb. Numb is not tranquil.

Our tranquility has also been disrupted in recent years, also repeatedly, by protests and riots after black men died in encounters with the police, killed with guns, Tasers, chokeholds, or beatings. Racial bias and excess force have been reported over many decades in myriad places around the country. Today, though, bystanders have cell phone cameras, and social media amplifies anger and accelerates organizing. Soon after Michael Brown was shot in Ferguson, Missouri, protesters around the country were marching with their hands in the air, chanting "Hands up. Don't shoot."

Citizen Dividends might inspire us to chant "Hands out. Let's connect." Hands out for handshakes, high fives, fist bumps, hugs.

Let's connect black and white and brown, poor and rich, cops and regular folks and elected officials. Then we may truly know domestic tranquility.

Provide for the common defense: Our Constitution was written by veterans. Many, most notably George Washington, were veterans of the battlefields; others of the political and diplomatic struggles to raise funds and recruit soldiers. They defined the military's role, powers, and limits. And they decided to have no standing army.

Today, U.S. military spending surpasses the next seven countries combined. Our military maintains 700 overseas bases; all other countries have a total of 30.[24]

The war in Afghanistan began in October 2001; fighting continues, and the Taliban again control large areas. The Bush administration unleashed "shock and awe" at Saddam Hussein in March 2003; the Iraq war and U.S. occupation brought forth ISIS and a surge in terrorism around the world. Syria is central today, with fighting also in Yemen, Sudan, Somalia, Nigeria, and other countries. America is involved in many places, with drone aircraft that drop bombs and launch missiles. After every U.S. airstrike, anywhere, militant Islamists escalate their efforts and recruit additional followers. Our government is preparing and planning for, and perhaps provoking, perpetual war.

We can provide for our defense at home by promoting basic income abroad. Let's ask residents of Afghanistan, Iraq, Syria, Libya, and Yemen if they want a version of this plan, and perhaps offer to help pay for it. Where the situation is unstable, it can be implemented in one town or city at a time. Residents are the only folks who can truly pacify a place, and residents will demand effective governments, with police, courts, schools, and commerce. This is a strategy to win people's hearts and minds and hands.

America is the world's number one economic superpower. When peace is our priority – truly, not mere rhetoric – we can deploy our economic might. One option is to redirect foreign aid, starting with military aid, possibly putting the money in escrow until a country enacts a version of basic income. Another option is to impose trade sanctions, or offer to remove current sanctions, or renegotiate trade agreements and perhaps rescind or withhold preferred trade status.

Consider these possibilities:

- Iran, to prod them to end support for Shia militants, particularly Hamas and Hezbollah.
- Saudi Arabia, to prod them to end support for Sunni militants and Wahhabi extremists.
- Pakistan, to promote their efforts to eliminate terrorism and safeguard nuclear materials.
- Turkey, to protect Kurds and other minorities, and to prevent a collapse of their uncertain democracy.
- Russia, to press for full withdrawal from Ukraine, and to preclude incursions into the Baltic countries or any others.
- China, to prevent military expansion in the South China Sea. Also to prod them to press North Korea to abandon nuclear weapons and missiles.

The Middle East, too, with America pressing both sides. In Israel, basic income will boost political unity and national security. Palestinians will have added means and reasons to halt all terrorist attacks and to create a stable, peaceful state. On both sides, therefore, residents and governments will be prepared to work actively toward enduring peace.

Boldly pursue peace around the world, to provide for the common defense.

Promote the general welfare: The Founders' phrase has been redefined, and now represents relentless efforts to create jobs and promote economic growth.

Our government mainly promotes the specific welfare, through programs that help special interests and selected individuals. Special interests get tax credits, subsidies, loan guarantees, and government contracts. Selected individuals get food stamps, TANF, housing support, and related assistance. The rest of us – the middle class, the majority – get promises about creating jobs and stimulating economic growth. Normally, though, that's all we get, promises.

Our Constitution doesn't mention *jobs* or *economic growth*.

Let's respect our Constitution and enact Citizen Dividends — a simple, direct, efficient way to promote the general welfare.

And secure the blessings of liberty to ourselves and our posterity: Liberty is an unalienable right, the Founders declared, a blessing, though they also stated that securing it requires a democratic government. They looked to the future, and dedicated their lives to creating a great nation.

Present-day politicians often talk about the future, but their rhetoric is refuted by a readiness to do whatever it takes to win the next election. America is declining. Our liberty is waning, and may soon be lost or eclipsed.

As individuals and together, We the People have to reestablish a responsible government that secures the blessings of liberty to ourselves and our posterity.

Do ordain and establish this Constitution.

* * * * *

The Bill of Rights renewed: When the Founders sent the Constitution to the states to be ratified, people were dissatisfied. After decades of British rule and despotism, wary Americans worried that the new national government might abuse its powers. State conventions instructed their representatives to add "further declaratory and restrictive clauses." Congress authorized twelve amendments; ten were soon ratified by three-fourths of the states; and we got the Bill of Rights.[25]

The First Amendment protects our freedom of religion, free speech, a free press, and our right to assemble and protest peacefully. But rights are mere theories when people lack the means to assert and defend them. Today, too many of us are struggling to pay our bills, busy with everyday concerns, and consequently can't afford to act when our rights are violated or threatened.

The Second Amendment is a continuing controversy, with endless disputes and frequent lawsuits about its meaning, history, and consequences. What was a "well-regulated militia" then, and what does that mean today? Can specified guns be banned completely? When and where should people be allowed to carry guns, openly or concealed? Innocent people are shot every day, and political paralysis is partly to blame. When every American has Citizen Dividends, we may be much closer to consensus on these questions.

The Third Amendment reminds us of the abuses people endured during the colonial period. British soldiers would commandeer people's homes, and demand to be fed and quartered. In many countries today, people's homes can be destroyed in an instant by drones, missiles, or grenades. This amendment, therefore, and the history it evokes, might motivate us to call for basic income wherever there is war or terrorism.

The Fourth Amendment has renewed relevance due to modern information technologies. Government has immense powers to conduct surveillance, search our data, and invade our privacy. It also has a reason or pretext: terrorism. When we're afraid, privacy can seem like a luxury; many of us accept or invite infringements, and urge or demand obedience by other folks. Personal privacy is valuable. Individuals have to be vigilant. Vigilance requires effort and costs money.

The Fifth Amendment protects us from abuses by government prosecutors. It mandates a grand jury before charging anyone with a capital crime, and it prohibits charging anyone twice for the same offense. We cannot be compelled to testify against ourselves. Government cannot seize property without due process, and must pay compensation. But government officials sometimes get it wrong. Citizen Dividends will help empower us to protect our property and ourselves.

The Sixth Amendment concerns judicial practices, our rights to a speedy trial by an impartial jury, to confront witnesses, to present a defense, and to have counsel. Being charged with a crime can be financially and emotionally devastating; innocent people can be seriously harmed. Economic security may be a prerequisite for preparing and presenting a defense.

The Seventh Amendment addresses civil matters, and preserves our right to a trial by jury. But corporations routinely ask us to sign agreements for binding arbitration, and most of us sign, sometimes without reading. Arbitration sounds fair, right? But the playing field is not level. Corporations have big tax-deductible budgets for legal matters, with in-house counsel and continuing relationships with arbitration providers. Regular folks are mostly on our own.

The Eighth Amendment prohibits excessive bail and fines, and bans cruel and unusual punishment. But folks can be stuck in jail because they're poor and can't afford bail. That's cruel though not unusual, and it violates core values about equal justice. It's also expensive, with taxpayers picking up the tab. When every citizen has money for bail, fines, penalties, and legal fees, justice will be more equal and proper.

The Ninth Amendment says the people retain rights that are not explicitly enumerated in the Constitution. Our rights shall not be denied or disparaged.

The Tenth Amendment reserves to the states, or the people, the powers that are neither prohibited by the Constitution nor assigned by it to the United States.

The Ninth and Tenth Amendments express colonists' core concerns: people are primary, states are sovereign, and the federal government is strictly limited. Today, however, we're not so concerned and we're much more constrained. Throughout the 20th century and the early years of the 21st, our federal government grew larger, wealthier, and more intrusive, imposing elaborate rules and regulations through an array of agencies — an "administrative state." Can we reaffirm these amendments? Should we? What is the ideal blend or balance of powers between people, state governments, and our federal government? Conditions change and so must our answers. People and state and local governments are demanding greater sovereignty — and Citizen Dividends will facilitate thoughtful debates and meaningful reforms.

*   *   *   *   *

Neither our Constitution nor the Bill of Rights says anything about corporations. That silence, though, was not from ignorance. British corporations were active throughout the thirteen colonies, and many colonies were established by, and as, corporations. The Founders decided to leave corporate charters as a matter for the states.

The Boston Tea Party was partly a protest against a global corporation, the East India Company, which owned the tea. Colonists were enraged by taxes levied to subsidize the company: corporate welfare. Shareholders included King George III and members of Parliament: crony capitalism. British troops protected company profits and property: public-private partnerships. The Boston Tea Party, though uniquely dramatic, colorful, and memorable, was only one of many protests against British corporations.[26]

After winning independence and the right to govern themselves, Americans were vigilant. State legislatures publicly debated requests for corporate charters, and imposed strict limits on ownership, operations, and duration. Over the next few decades, however, as America industrialized, owners of corporations became wealthier and more politically powerful, and these trends accelerated with the Civil War. The Fourteenth Amendment was written to secure the rights of former slaves, ratified in 1868. Corporations promptly started citing it in lawsuits, claiming that they are "persons." One lawsuit reached the Supreme Court in 1886, and the Court accepted that claim. *Corporate personhood* is now established legal doctrine. Lawyers and judges invented it; elected representatives never explicitly authorized it. The Supreme Court affirmed and extended it in 2010 with *Citizens United*, when the Court decided that corporations can fund political campaigns without disclosure.[27]

Perhaps we should admit that our republic is lost, our democracy a pretense — that we are ruled by the rich, a plutocracy, and by big corporations, a corporatocracy.

Admit and accept it?

Or change it! We can wage – and win – a peaceful democratic revolution to rediscover, revitalize, and realize America's founding ideals and values: We the People renewed.

11. Our Strategy

Are you ready for basic income, at least a thoughtful debate? Or do you have more questions first?

A leap of faith may be required. This plan affects all aspects of our lives, our culture, our society, and our government, so it's beyond the scope of conventional analyses. But our political system is dysfunctional, and current policies are flawed or inadequate, sometimes counterproductive. Multiple problems are serious, getting worse, and causing irreversible harms to millions of people in the United States and billions around the world. We can leap or we will suffer.

One question is whether a state or city can enact a version. The answer is yes.

Alaskans have had a small basic income since 1982. Every resident gets an equal cash payment every year, the Permanent Fund Dividend. They love it. The benefits are well documented. Income inequality is lower in Alaska than any other state, and the PFD is the main reason. The amount varies, usually between $1,000 and $2,000 a year. Perhaps they'll expand it to create PFD Plus.*

Local programs were tested in a series of Income Maintenance Experiments between 1967 and 1974, funded by the federal Office of Economic Opportunity. In urban, suburban, and rural communities around the country, a total of 8,500 people got guaranteed monthly payments in addition to their earnings. Researchers tracked work hours, incomes, family status, and other variables. The final analyses showed a decline in total work hours of 6 to 13 percent, yet that decline was a positive sign. Women stayed home with their kids, teens stayed in school or went back to school, men left bad jobs to seek better ones. People did what was best for themselves and their families, and their choices were also good for society.

Americans, today, work many more hours than in the 1970s. In most families, both parents have to work full-time, often placing kids in daycare. Instead, everyone will have opportunities to seek better jobs, stay in school, be full-time parents, or just get more sleep. Folks who leave jobs will create openings for other workers. A voluntary decline of 6 percent would end involuntary unemployment.

A local experiment in Canada included a whole town, Dauphin, Manitoba. Between 1974 and 1979, poor residents got unconditional funds to cover basic expenses. The results: a steep drop in poverty, plus significantly improved health, higher employment, and better education outcomes.

---

* The money comes from oil royalties and investments; that's why the amount varies. Investments are diversified to outlast the oil; that's what makes it permanent. Recipients must be residents for more than six months of the year, and it includes children. In 2016, the PFD was $1,022. In 2015, it was a record, $2,072, which is $8,288 for a family of four.

The previous peak was $2,069 in 2008, and that year everyone also got a one-time bonus, $1,200, so a family of four got $13,076. Sarah Palin was the governor in 2008. She championed that bonus, the main reason for her high approval ratings. Thus, when John McCain selected Palin to run for vice president, the PFD was a major factor.

Another local program is ongoing. Since 1997, the Eastern Band of Cherokee Indians in North Carolina has distributed casino profits to all members of the tribe, including children. Researchers from Duke University have been studying the program, comparing recipients with residents of the surrounding community. The evidence "strongly suggests that on the whole, universal basic income works."[*]

Local programs can be enacted more quickly than a national plan. Regular folks generally understand local budgets and policies, and local officials are relatively accessible. Activists can attract allies by citing programs to cut, reform, or eliminate, and calculating the potential basic income. Then talk to friends, neighbors, etc., and offer a choice: Are you content with the status quo? Or would you rather have the money?

Every local effort, anywhere, helps move these ideas forward everywhere. Cities and states that act quickly are likely to become role models and tourist magnets.

Politics is personal: Democracy, when it's truly healthy, starts with regular folks and includes everyone. As equals, we decide what we want for our cities, our states, and our country. Then we select representatives to help us get what we want. Elected officials are public servants.

Our political system is "inverted." Elected officials are treated like VIPs (very important persons) and sometimes act like celebrities. Politics is reality TV. Politicians are the stars, performing roles that are mostly or entirely scripted; special interests are the writers,

---

[*] The Eastern Cherokee program is in Appendix 1, along with more about the Permanent Fund Dividend and the Income Maintenance Experiments. The Dauphin experiment is in Appendix 3. Local programs have also been tested in Namibia, India, and other countries, each time with remarkably positive outcomes, and those are in Appendix 3 as well.

directors, producers, and advertisers. The rest of us, regular folks, are the audience. Our only responsibility, and only at scheduled intervals, is to give a thumbs up or thumbs down.[28]

We have to reclaim our proper role. Regular folks have the power to hire – and fire – elected officials and special interests. We the People are the real executive producers, and Citizen Dividends will be monthly reminders of our role and our power.

Liberal? Conservative? The best of both! Before we're liberals or conservatives, and before we're Democrats or Republicans, we're Americans. More fundamentally, of course, we're human beings. Our humanity defines us and unites us. Political labels distract and divide us.

In conventional discourse, *liberal* means pro-government, while *conservative* is anti-government and pro-market or pro-business. But thoughtful liberals know that government can be abusive, intrusive, and ineffective. And thoughtful conservatives know that we need government to protect personal liberty and keep our communities safe. The labels' flaws are most evident when we consider Social Security and Medicare. "Liberals" are fighting to preserve the status quo, so they're the conservatives on these issues. "Conservatives" want to abolish or privatize the programs; that's not conservative, it's retrograde or reactionary.

Current policies, moreover, are mainly *neoliberal* or *neoconservative*. Neoliberal economic policies actively use government to promote markets and private businesses; that's why we have corporate welfare. Neoconservative foreign policies endorse military interventions to expand markets and impose American values; that's how we got the wars in Afghanistan and Iraq, and it's why our government botched those wars. Neoliberal is not liberal. Neoconservative is not

conservative. Both ideologies and both sets of policies enrich big corporations – CEOs, shareholders, lobbyists, et al. – while disregarding
and often harming regular folks.

The labels are distractions, often useless and sometimes harmful;
we should shed or avoid them. Let's start with personal preferences
and state them clearly, simply, directly. You might want a large basic
income to maximize personal liberty, to cut government deeply and
quickly, or to ensure that all parents can provide for their kids. You
might favor a smaller amount to keep taxes low, to launch the plan
promptly, or to preserve incentives to work and earn. Shed the labels,
start and stay with personal preferences, and we'll be more ready to
compromise and more likely to succeed.

Labels and ideologies should also be irrelevant when we're cutting, reforming, and eliminating current programs. Our preferences
will mainly reflect personal circumstances, our age, family, finances,
and so on. With corporate welfare, everyone wants to eliminate that
spending, or so we say. Instead of labels, unique individuals with personal dreams, goals, values, and concerns.

The best of both, liberal and conservative, Americans working
together to realize our common interests.

We the People versus the status quo: Politics today is left versus
right, liberals versus conservatives, Democrats versus Republicans.
Our movement will be regular folks versus special interests and the
status quo.

Imagine a party primary, Democratic or Republican, for a local,
state, or national office. Suppose one candidate calls for Citizen
Dividends, while others tout the party's usual platform and policies.
Proponents will claim, accurately, that they represent voters' core
values.

Democrats can quote Franklin Roosevelt's call for "a second Bill of Rights" that establishes "a new basis of security and prosperity … for all — regardless of station, race, or creed." They can cite Lyndon Johnson on civil rights, the Great Society, and the War on Poverty, and show how basic income will advance these causes. Also Martin Luther King Jr.: "The solution to poverty is to abolish it directly by a now widely discussed measure: the guaranteed income." Democrats want government action to reduce global warming, and a preferred approach is a carbon tax and dividend; this plan simply puts the dividend first.

Republicans can refer to Ronald Reagan on freedom, free enterprise, individual initiative, and cutting the federal government, presenting Citizen Dividends as a plan to realize Reagan's vision. Tax cuts are a top priority for most Republicans, and many favor a flat tax. One way to make a flat tax practical and popular – probably the only way – is to combine it with basic income. An early champion of the flat tax was economist Milton Friedman, who wrote "We should replace the ragbag of specific welfare programs with a single comprehensive program of income supplements in cash — a negative income tax."

Now imagine a general election where one party campaigns for this plan — one party only. Proponents can quote the other party's stated goals, values, and campaign materials: "If that's what you want, vote for me." Proponents might also denounce the other party's candidates as agents or tools of the special interests, or as liars or fools. Landslide victories are likely.

A three-way race might have an independent proponent running against two major party candidates with their usual platforms. Independents can educate voters about the 1960s, when moderate

Democrats and moderate Republicans supported guaranteed income — and can then attack both parties for dropping the idea and betraying regular folks. The status quo is bipartisan. This plan is perfect for independent campaigns.

"Third" parties can craft versions as vehicles for their values. Some parties are religious, and can highlight biblical injunctions to provide for the poor. Some parties are socialist, and might emphasize prospects for worker-owned business cooperatives. The Green Party already endorses basic income, and has included it in the platform since 2004. Libertarians can underscore the gains in personal liberty, and perhaps cite Friedrich Hayek's support for "the security of a minimum income." A current third party might soon be second or first.

Basic income proponents from any party – or independents – can present themselves as the true voices for hope, change, reform, and progress, while calling on all Americans to work together as We the People.

A peaceful democratic revolution: The Declaration of Independence proclaims government's core purpose: to secure our unalienable rights to life, liberty, and the pursuit of happiness. But our government is broken, and has subjected us to "a long train of abuses and usurpations, pursuing invariably the same object."

Our Constitution includes a mandate to promote the general welfare, and members of Congress take an oath: "I do solemnly swear (or affirm) that I will support and defend the Constitution of the United States against all enemies, foreign and domestic." But current policies plainly promote the special welfare, selected special interests, primarily the special *wealthfare*, wealthy individuals and corporations.

America today is a plutocracy, corporatocracy, or special-interest-ocracy.

The Founders didn't act alone. The first American revolution was fought by regular folks. They were pursuing happiness, liberty, equality, and justice. They willingly served and sacrificed. And they succeeded.

Now is our time to make history.

12. Now

The Declaration of Independence concludes with these words:

> And for the support of this Declaration, with a firm reliance on the protection of divine providence, we mutually pledge to each other our lives, our fortunes, and our sacred honor.

Signers knew the risks. If captured by the British, they would have been executed for treason.

Sign-on for Citizen Dividends, and we'll have lasting rewards: our lives will improve, our fortunes will increase, and our honor will flourish.

Attracting allies: What is the America you want to live in, say in five or ten years? What are your dreams for your children and grandchildren? Would you like $1,000 a month as a guaranteed income for the rest of your life?

Hope is attractive and these questions inspire it, inviting folks to envision a desired future. Questions are most constructive when we listen actively, respectfully, with follow-up questions and dialogue. Most politicians only pretend to listen. They routinely incite fear and distrust, not hope: be afraid if my opponent wins, don't believe what he or she says. They're also mired in nostalgia. Democrats love New

Deal and Great Society programs, while Republicans revere Ronald Reagan and promise to take us back to a better time, to "make America great again." Both parties are constantly looking in the rearview mirror, driving with their foot on the brakes.

With this plan, we can drive confidently toward a more just, peaceful, and prosperous future. When we're confident, especially when we're also civil and joyful, folks will want to join us.

We can – indeed should, or at least aspire to – view everyone as potential allies, likely to endorse basic income once they understand it. Understanding requires time, however, and as Thomas Paine wrote in *Common Sense*, "Time makes more converts than reason." Let's also remember that feelings come first, normally. When folks feel good, hopeful, and respected, they'll be eager to understand.

Attracting is very different from recruiting, persuading, convincing, or enrolling. Attracting is easier, especially if we use stories, music, theater, and videos. We're laying the foundations for a healthy democracy, so we should start with friends, family, and neighbors — personal and local. Young folks included, even those who are not yet old enough to vote, encouraging them to be active citizens. Also folks who are turned off or turned away from politics, or were never turned on; they may be most impatient to overthrow the status quo.

To sustain our confidence, and to renew it after setbacks, we should meet periodically with friends and allies to share stories, strategies, tactics, and hugs. Community is comforting and uplifting, as many of us know from attending religious services. Gathering together is valuable even when we're preaching to the choir. Meetings are opportunities to learn the words and the music, and to rehearse, so we can sing on key and make a joyful noise.

A good tactic for attracting allies is to talk about the flaws and failures with current policies, particularly about jobs. Millions of us have jobs that are threatened or endangered – or already lost – due to robots, computers, 3-D printing, voice recognition, artificial intelligence, and related technologies. Driverless cars will soon replace millions of truck drivers, taxi drivers, and Uber drivers. Over the next decade, we'll see increasing job losses and disruptions among accountants, journalists, lawyers, and doctors. Many professional jobs can now be performed remotely, in India for instance, places where workers are paid much less than Americans. Those jobs aren't coming back.

Another tactic is to question conventional notions about our partisan political system. When we read or hear anything about left versus right or liberal versus conservative, we can present this alternative — the best of both. Send emails, phone talk radio, speak out at public events, post comments on social media, compose songs and create videos, and write letters to the editors of newspapers and magazines. Every contact is another potential ally.

In our conversations, emails, etc., we ought to emphasize the moral basis for these ideas. Moral arguments are central to the Declaration of Independence, and were fundamental for the successful movements that abolished slavery, won the right for women to vote, enacted civil rights laws in the 1960s, and achieved marriage equality for gays and lesbians. The moral imperative with this plan is obvious: basic human rights – justice, liberty, dignity, and a baseline of equality – for everyone. For most Americans, morality includes patriotism, so let's be sure to highlight the patriotic aspects.

Educating ourselves: Through campaigning for these ideas, we're learning that our government truly is ours. Learning to act as

citizens, not merely consumers, customers, clients, critics, or spectators. Learning that politics can be meaningful and satisfying.

Our learning can include reading about related ideas from
Thomas Jefferson, Thomas Paine, the Progressive era, the origin of
Social Security, and so on. Reviewing the history helps us stay moti-
vated. Telling the story is a way to attract allies.*

One lesson from this history is to postpone committing to the
details. The Townsend Plan and Share Our Wealth called for sums
that seemed excessive, imprudent, unaffordable. Critics had ammu-
nition to attack or ridicule the plans and proponents. Potential allies
were deterred.

Richard Nixon's Family Assistance Plan and George McGovern's
Demogrants were fiscally sound, written and vetted by prominent
economists, but blocked through political maneuvers. This is the
second lesson: compromise. Nixon's plan was denounced by welfare rights groups who said the amount was too small; if activists
had endorsed, it would have passed, then the activists could have
campaigned for increases or local supplements. McGovern's proposal was opposed by labor unions that mainly sought job guarantees for their members; instead, unions might have underscored the
universal benefits, and used that emphasis to expand their mem-
bership. Political maneuvers, though less public and more personal,
also blocked Jimmy Carter's Program for Better Jobs and Income
Support.

---

* To assist with learning and telling the story, Appendix 1 is chronological and
includes many quotes. When talking with liberals, start with Franklin Roosevelt,
Lyndon Johnson, and Martin Luther King Jr. With conservatives, cite Friedrich
Hayek, Milton Friedman, and other Nobel laureate economists. With CEOs and
entrepreneurs, mention Peter Drucker, Jeremy Rifkin, and venture investors in
Silicon Valley. With religious folks, talk about the Bible and its edicts to love and
serve the poor; also Philip Wogaman. With secular folks, quote Robert Theobald,
Erich Fromm, and Buckminster Fuller.

Third: a mass movement is imperative. Populists and Progressives achieved major reforms in the early 1900s, enacting policies we take for granted. Millions of Americans supported the Townsend Plan and Share Our Wealth in 1935, and they generated the political will to enact Social Security. Mass protests won big victories in the 1960s, and civil rights organizers were expanding their efforts, demanding action to end poverty, though the movement lost momentum after Martin Luther King Jr. was killed. There were no marches, rallies, or demonstrations in support of Nixon's plan or McGovern's or Carter's.

The summary lesson: We the People win when we're smart, strategic, and resolute.

Educating ourselves can also start with specific issues or problems. Select immigration, say, or education, health care, etc., and consider the current situation. Who's affected? What's happening? Are we okay with that? Then contrast current policies with this basic income alternative, imagining and thinking about what we can expect. Benefits will be obvious, even if the basic income is local, not national, and the issue or problem is remote. For example, after a flood, earthquake, or hurricane, folks will have funds to help relatives and refugees.*

You might join or start a group, choose one issue each week or month, and discuss it at public meetings or potluck dinners. Talk about what you can achieve with a local basic income, and what to demand in a national plan. Consider the amount, program cuts, tax

---

* Floods, etc., are added reasons to act quickly; the next event might be tomorrow. In every natural disaster, the greatest harm is to the poor. Inequities were evident in the Baton Rouge flood in 2016 and Hurricane Sandy in 2012. Hurricane Katrina hit New Orleans in 2005, yet countless folks are still financially underwater. With Citizen Dividends, even the poorest will have money to prepare, to flee if necessary, and then to recover and move forward.

reforms, and other details. Review strategies and tactics, and say what you personally will do or contribute.

Organizing actively: Public events are opportunities to reach out to politicians, journalists, educators, clergy, and other potential allies. Invite them to share their ideas and opinions, or just to learn.

Politicians are likely to praise the plan and proponents, but refuse to commit; they're politicians, and vague promises are standard practice. Our first goal is simply to get them to say the words *basic income* or *Citizen Dividends* (or *UBI, guaranteed income, negative income tax,* or other term). They'll be on the record. We can quote them when we talk with friends, on social media, to journalists, and so on. Perhaps their opponents will be more courageous.

Some politicians will want to see polls, petitions, or other signs of public support, and some will conduct their own polls. Polls and petitions can be persuasive, though we have to read the fine print. Special interests will also be polling and petitioning, and will inflate costs, distort details, and exaggerate the number of folks who will quit jobs or misuse the money. Then they'll publicize their "data" to amplify doubts, disputes, and disagreements.

Some politicians will propose pilot projects. That seems positive and prudent, a way to assess possibilities and evaluate variations. Yet we already know the auspicious outcomes from the Income Maintenance Experiments in the 1960s and '70s. We can also be guided by recent or current programs in Canada, Finland, Holland, India, and elsewhere, including privately-funded projects in the United States.[29]

Is another pilot project really necessary? Or is that a delaying tactic? Politicians are timid, typically, and elected officials constantly worry about losing support from the special interests that funded their prior campaigns. Delay is costly. Millions of Americans are hungry or homeless. Calling for a pilot, in effect, is telling vulnerable folks that we don't trust them, don't respect them, and won't help them until someday later or never. In the time it would take to conduct any pilot, we could end hunger, end homelessness, end extreme poverty, and make real progress on many other issues.

We might just start small – a basic income of $200 or $300 a month – then use polls and petitions, and the next election, to ask if people want to undo it, keep it small, or expand it. Polls, petitions, and elections will also be necessary, of course, for deciding details about program cuts, tax reforms, and so on.*

Organizing requires folks who are willing to lead. Let's cultivate leaders among our friends and allies and ourselves, becoming leaders. The main requirements are desire or passion and commitment. Leaders might also be elected officials who join our parade, earn our respect, and make their way to the front.

As potential leaders arise, emerge, or join us, we want folks who are true public servants. Some would-be leaders are wannabe celebrities; some celebrities are wannabe leaders; and sometimes we confuse the two, mistaking celebrities for leaders while treating leaders as celebrities. True leaders seek to inspire and encourage everyone to act together as We the People. True public servants respect personal dreams and goals.

---

* One option for a small or simple start is to keep the current tax code with a slight change. Either expand the EITC and similar tax credits, to make them "fully refundable," so the money also goes to people who have no jobs and no income. Or replace the standard deduction with a fully refundable credit. A bill to do the latter, the Tax Cut for the Rest of Us Act of 2006, was introduced in Congress but never debated.

Then, perhaps one step at a time, enact tax reforms, program cuts, and other changes — an incremental strategy and a gradual revolution.

Mobilizing politically: Mobilizing is partly to elect or re-elect our allies. Beyond elections – before, during, and after – we'll be doing what we must to force government to act.

We can build on the efforts and successes of the Tea Party, Occupy, and Black Lives Matter. Their anti-status-quo anger is ours, as well, and our plan can be theirs. Activists from each of these movements – and many other groups too, of course, on a wide range of issues – might endorse basic income to advance their causes. They may be eager to join us in organizing rallies, marches, sit-ins, media alerts, and related actions. They might be our champions as candidates in the next election.

As we approach any election, we'll be less concerned with attracting politicians and more inclined to confront them: endorse basic income, or we'll denounce you as an obstacle to progress, a cause of major problems, or an agent of special interests. Maybe they'll join us. Maybe they'll refuse and lose, then reassess and reemerge as our allies.

Every vote for any version of this plan is a step forward. We have to be willing to switch parties, at least one-time-only. Too many of us have been too loyal for too long, while the two major parties have been too self-serving. A readiness to switch parties, or to challenge and change a party from within, is vital for a healthy democracy.

Elections might have several proponents calling for distinct versions. We'll have lively debates and a likely imminent victory.

Writing the bill: One way to attract and educate allies is to draft a bill. Activists can highlight that term, draft, then invite folks to discuss it and suggest revisions. With the first draft and first bill, our main goal is to build consensus.

A local bill might be a statement of support, calling for a national program. Or a statement of intent, a step toward enacting a local or state version. Initial bills might be rather general or quite specific for the moment and jurisdiction.

Ballot initiatives are powerful tools, perfect for our purposes. Citizens can draft a proposal, collect signatures, and get their idea onto the ballot. If it passes, it's the law. This is an option in 24 states, the District of Columbia, and many cities, and activists might make it a priority tactic. With an initiative on the ballot, politicians, pundits, and interest groups are compelled to comment: for or against, they'll publicize the plan. If it wins, politicians who supported it are likely to also win. An initiative anywhere, even if it's defeated, can produce far-reaching gains in building our movement.*

Local and state governments have to balance their budgets each year. Those bills and ballot initiatives may be required to specify the sources of funds (program cuts, tax reforms, block grants from the jurisdiction(s) above, etc.) along with any necessary waivers, approvals, or enabling legislation from the jurisdiction(s) above. The basic income might be fairly small or only a goal. Or it might vary with economic conditions, like the Alaska PFD.

Our national government can coin money and run deficits. The first bill can simply set an amount, say $500 or $750 or $1,000 a month, and a flat tax rate, say 15, 20, 25, or 30 percent. Those are details, we can compromise. Let's act promptly and enact this core plan. Then we can focus on cutting, reforming, or eliminating programs. Those

---

* Millions of folks first heard about basic income in October 2013, after activists submitted signatures for a ballot referendum in Switzerland. Their campaign was widely reported in the United States. Many news accounts mentioned Milton Friedman, Martin Luther King Jr., the Family Assistance Plan, or the Permanent Fund Dividen. A few reports considered prospects for reviving the idea.

cuts and reforms will be relatively easy after the core plan is in place, and are nearly impossible today.

Passing the law: One or two elected officials can introduce a bill in a city council, state legislature, or the U.S. Congress. With a bill on the table, organizing and mobilizing are much easier; this is why we want current officials to join our movement. When it's introduced, we'll celebrate with rallies and through the media, praising the sponsors, seeking co-sponsors, and pressing party leaders to move the bill forward.

With any bill(s) anywhere, though even before we have one, our movement is likely to grow quickly, perhaps exponentially. We saw the swift rise of the Tea Party, Occupy, and Black Lives Matter, and this plan can attract, excite, and unite folks who supported any of them. The Tea Party started in spring 2009, and elected many supporters in 2010. Our movement might have a huge impact on the next election.

The next election may be soon, a special election to fill a vacant office. Special elections are great opportunities for us. Schedules are tight, turnout normally low. Campaigns can be referendums, basic income versus the status quo. With every election, special and general, we'll refine our strategies, tactics, and rhetoric as we prepare for future victories.

Candidates in diverse parties might offer distinct versions — or the same version, while emphasizing different goals, features, and priorities.

- Donald Trump promised to "drain the swamp." Republicans can highlight plans to cut taxes, shrink government, rescind regulations, and dethrone special interests.

- Democrats can emphasize social and economic justice, uniting diverse constituents while appealing anew to folks who abandoned the party in recent elections.
- Greens, Libertarians, and independents can focus on political reforms that are truly nonpartisan or transpartisan, to empower citizens and strengthen our democracy.

Passing the law will be relatively simple where our elected allies are a majority, though if they're in diverse parties we may have to mobilize to compel compromise. Where only a few officials are allies, we'll employ greater force, with rallies, sit-ins, strikes, and such. Mass protests are most effective when people have specific demands, in our case to pass this law and implement it immediately. A rally or sit-in might surround a city council, a state capitol, or the U.S. Capitol while officials are in session — and keep them there until they act.

*   *   *   *   *

In the 2016 election, Donald Trump and Hillary Clinton were speaking to different voters, proclaiming different values, presenting different policies, campaigning as if we were two different countries. Each attacked and ridiculed the other. Both claimed that they knew what was best for everyone, and would do what was best, as our champions, heroes, and saviors. Voter turnout was the lowest in 20 years, only 55 percent. But neither Trump nor Clinton was the problem. Both were products and symptoms of our failing political system.

After the election, and partly because of it, system failures are far more obvious — and far more serious, even dangerous.

Citizen Dividends will be monthly reminders that we are citizens, and equal; that we live in one country, united; and that we have reasons to work together, We the People. Instead of trusting Trump, Clinton, or any politician, regular folks will decide what we want, we'll tell elected officials what to do, and we'll hold them accountable.

Basic income is only a first step. Our political system has been failing for decades, our government broken in countless ways. Too many of us are struggling with debts, worrying about our retirement prospects, worrying about our kids and how they'll manage. Most of us are upset or angry about crime, taxes, health care, immigration, global warming, national security, or other issues. We've got a lot of work to do.

This plan will transform our politics. When our national government distributes the money, it'll redistribute political power. Regular folks everywhere will see, and appreciate, that politics is personal and local. Every American will have direct incentives to cooperate and compromise. We want and deserve – and we can have – lean, effective, responsive government at all levels. We can have a politics of consensus and conviviality.

*   *   *   *   *

What do you think?

Do these ideas make sense?

Are you ready to help make history?

We could have a basic income, the money in our hands, within a year or two. A peaceful democratic revolution for personal dignity, liberty, justice, and peace.

From the Author

In the Introduction, I asked you to pretend we're friends who haven't seen each other in a while, perhaps not since high school, and to imagine that this book was inspired by our shared concerns. That's how I've been thinking about you.

Before I began writing, *politics is personal* was an abstract concept. It became concrete through seeing you as a friend and seeking to connect. I've been actively imagining multiple diverse versions of "you," unique individuals with distinct dreams, goals, and concerns. While reading, did you feel included and respected? I hope so.

To help you appreciate these ideas, I kept it brief. And I've been extra careful to be accurate with the economics, politics, history, and facts about recent events. If you believe I've been too brief, and if you find any errors or omissions or anything out-of-date, please publish your comments so I and other folks can learn from you.

You might think I'm too optimistic – or naïve or foolish – and too quick to conjecture, leaping to conclusions without adequate evidence or analysis. Perhaps you feel that I too often repeat myself. Optimism, conjecture, and repetition are necessary, I believe, to cut through the constant downpour of noise, nonsense, and negativity in the news. My optimism, in part, is cheerleading.

Also in the Introduction I stated that "my identity and background ought to be irrelevant." One reason was to make it easier for you to imagine that we're friends. Another, to keep the book short and straightforward, not padded with narrative or anecdotes about me. Third, to help me – force me, actually – to focus on you. Most important, to help you consider these ideas directly, candidly, without biases or prejudices that might deter you – or anyone – from reading. I want everyone to feel welcome.

My aim is to be truly nonpartisan or transpartisan. The 2016 election, for me, was an extreme, extended test of my ideas, beliefs, and assumptions. This manuscript was nearly complete when the campaigns started, and I revised it while observing the candidates and their supporters, seeking to appreciate all sides — while also trying to identify my biases, and to counter or delete statements that might be misinterpreted. Yet I'm sure I still have blind spots and I request your forbearance.

Friends have warned me to expect personal attacks. If anyone attacks, I hope you'll defend me. Please. Personal attacks, in my opinion, are evidence that the attacker is bound or blinded by self-interest, or an agent of some special interest. Personal attacks are a sign and a cause of dysfunctional politics.

I invite disputes about issues. Do you identify as a fierce liberal or a strict conservative? In 2016, did you strongly support – or strongly oppose – Donald Trump? What do you think today about the Trump administration, about the Republican-controlled Congress, and about where we're heading as a country?

Let's talk, debate, dispute, even quarrel — though with mutual respect, while actively seeking places where we agree. Is there a version of this plan you might endorse? Are you willing to compromise, so we can move forward?

When I mentioned high school in the Introduction and above, I was recalling friends from those years. We wanted to create a better world and we weren't embarrassed to say so. More than that, we believed we could and would. I see similar idealism today. Young folks can lead the movement for basic income, and perhaps they must; they have the most to lose if the status quo persists, and the most to gain from our success. Older folks should encourage the young by respectfully listening.

Through writing this book, I learned to be extra wary of conventional discourse, particularly the word *we*. As I stated in Chapter 1, *we* is often deceptive, coercive, or self-serving. When politicians, pundits, CEOs, and other public figures say *"we,"* I now have an internal alarm, a voice that says "There is no *we.*" Then it prods me with questions: Who, specifically, is the speaker talking about? Does that "we" include me? Did I consent? Do I consent? Did other folks consent? If there was no active consent, I discount, dismiss, or challenge whatever the person said.

I also learned to eschew abstract concepts, especially *the market* and *the economy*, examples from Chapter 5. Abstract language is dehumanizing and dangerous. I encourage you to join me in questioning vague or abstract terms — and confronting folks who use them, ideally educating those folks.

In the final section of Chapter 10, I implied that corporate welfare, crony capitalism, and public-private partnerships are similar to the policies England imposed on the colonies before 1776. That's accurate, in my opinion. British troops collected taxes, and corporations profited. The colonists rebelled against both King George III and the corporations.*

Our political system is more partisan, polarized, and paralyzed in 2017 than a year ago, before the election, and far worse than when I conceived the book in early 2011. Even so, writing this book renewed my respect for democracy. I'm now more confident that regular folks are capable of governing ourselves. And more certain that we must. Confident and certain, sincerely, though I'm also more aware of the challenges and obstacles.

Now, after repeatedly asking what you think and what you want, and after several years of considering you a friend, I feel obliged to share my answers. I favor a fairly large basic income, at least $1,000 a month, plus local supplements. More important though, I want it soon, ASAP, even if it's only $100. Looking back at my life, I see many times when any amount would have freed me to make better choices, probably leading to greater success and more happiness. Thus, I haven't been focusing only on you. This book is personal, it's about me, too.

I want to cut government deeply, while protecting everyone who depends on current programs. *Do no harm.* Basic income first.

A consensus rate for a flat tax is likely to be between 15 and 30 percent, as in the tables in Chapter 3, and I'd accept a higher rate, even 35 or 40 percent. I endorse a VAT and financial transaction taxes, and suggest we postpone debates about payroll taxes, estate taxes, and corporate taxes. I strongly support taxes on fossil fuels

---

* Before they rebelled, the colonists endured years of abuse. The Declaration of Independence cites a few dozen violations, and acknowledges that "mankind are more disposed to suffer, while evils are sufferable, than to right themselves by abolishing the forms to which they are accustomed." We've endured decades of government by special interests, for special interests — specifically by and for superrich individuals and big corporations. How long will we suffer? When will we rebel?

and other takings, with land value taxes as the main or sole source of funds for local governments.

On most issues, however, aside from what I've already written, I prefer to be quiet. Issues are complicated, respected authorities disagree, and, frankly, in many cases I'm not yet sure what I think. Though I am ready to speak out on one topic: The best way to defend America, I'm certain, is to actively pursue peace and disarmament — and to invite, entice, encourage, or pressure other countries to enact basic income programs.

Ideas are to inspire action, I believe. Talking, writing, reading, and listening are valuable and often necessary for deciding what to do and preparing to do it. Yet ideas are most meaningful when we apply them, doing something new or different.

This movement requires thousands of leaders, maybe millions — maybe you. I want to live in a true democracy, without leaving the country, and that means I'm counting on you. I hope we'll be allies and friends in the successful campaign for Citizen Dividends.

Now is your time to say what you want for yourself, your family, your community, and your country. And it's our time to act together as We the People.

Appendix 1:
Related Ideas and Efforts

Biblical Origins

The Bible commands us to do justice, to show mercy, and to provide for the poor. To do unto others as we would have them do unto us. And, in Leviticus, to forgive debts and redistribute property:

> You shall make the fiftieth year holy, and proclaim liberty throughout the land to all its inhabitants. It shall be a jubilee for you, and each of you shall return to his own property, and each of you shall return to his family.

This passage reminds us of the link between liberty and property. For liberty, everyone needs food and shelter, property, therefore property must sometimes be redistributed. "Proclaim liberty throughout the land" is inscribed on the Liberty Bell, which rang in Philadelphia to announce the signing of the Declaration of Independence.

The gospels include many parables of Jesus aiding and comforting the poor. He fed the masses through the miracle of the loaves and fishes, and didn't require people to dig ditches or wash dishes. He commanded us to follow his example and to love our neighbors.

In biblical times, and throughout most human history, people lived in extended families or clans and interacted with their neighbors every day. Neighbors depended on each other.

We now live in nuclear families, parents and kids only. Many of us live alone. Nearly everyone has neighbors we've never met.

One way to aid, comfort, and love our neighbors is to provide them with a basic income. Does this plan fulfill the biblical commandments? Must charity be direct and personal as well, loving our neighbors and looking in their eyes? Good questions. We might pray for guidance.

Initial Ideas

Thomas More may have been the first to suggest that society should help the poor. *Utopia* (1516) portrayed an imaginary ideal society. Writing about crime and punishment, he asserted that "it would be far more to the point to provide everyone with some means of livelihood, so that nobody's under the frightful necessity of becoming, first a thief, and then a corpse."

In a 1525 essay, "On Assistance To The Poor," **Ludovico Vives** reasoned that the state is responsible for providing some minimum of financial support for all residents. Public officials are in the best position to identify the poor who require relief, he maintained, so they are the ones who should be in charge of providing assistance. His ideas influenced legislation in England, Germany, and belatedly in Bruges, Belgium, where he wrote the essay at the request of government officials.

America's Founders

Thomas Jefferson, while serving in the Virginia legislature before writing the Declaration of Independence, proposed giving 50 acres of land to any propertyless individual willing to farm it. The purpose was to secure people's subsistence and their rights as citizens.

He discussed the idea in a letter to James Madison on October 28, 1785:

> The earth is given as a common stock for man to labour and live on. ... It is too soon yet in our country to say that every man who cannot find employment but who can find uncultivated land, shall be at liberty to cultivate it, paying a moderate rent. But it is not too soon to provide by every possible means that as few as possible shall be without a little portion of land. The small landholders are the most precious part of a state.

John Adams, the second U.S. president, asserted that "every member of society" should be "possessed of small estates" as a basis for "equal liberty."

James Madison, the primary author of the U.S. Constitution, and the fourth president, endorsed the idea of enacting laws to "raise extreme indigence towards a state of comfort."

Thomas Paine is most remembered as the author of *Common Sense,* his 1776 pamphlet calling for American independence. In *Agrarian Justice* (1797), he described land as the "common heritage of mankind," and proposed to have landowners pay a "ground rent" into a "national fund." Every citizen would then receive a cash payment at age 21 and yearly payments starting at age 50. "A right, and not a charity."

His title page summarized the idea:

> Agrarian justice, opposed to agrarian law, and to agrarian monopoly. Being a plan for meliorating the conditions of man by creating in every nation, a national fund, to pay to every person, when arriving at the age of twenty-one years, the sum of fifteen pounds sterling, to enable him or her to begin the world! And also, ten pounds sterling per annum during life to every person

now living of the age of fifty years, and to all others when they shall arrive at that age, to enable them to live in old age without wretchedness, and go decently out of the world.

Seniors will "see before them the certainty of escaping the miseries that under other governments accompany old age." Democracy will "have an advocate and an ally in the heart of all nations."

Paine's plan anticipates Henry George and the land value tax, the Alaska Permanent Fund and Permanent Fund Dividend, and proposals from many modern economists.

Mid to Late 1800s

English philosopher and economist John Stuart Mill published *Principles of Political Economy* in 1848. That was a year of revolution in France, Germany, Denmark, Hungary, and other European countries; also the year Karl Marx published *The Communist Manifesto*. Partly in response to those events, Mill issued a second edition in 1849. There he endorsed a form of socialism that "does not contemplate the abolition of private property, nor even of inheritance," though with the distribution

> a certain minimum is first assigned for the subsistence of every member of the community, whether capable or not of labour. The remainder of the produce is shared in certain proportions, to be determined beforehand, among the three elements, Labour, Capital, and Talent.

His book was widely used as an economics textbook into the early 1900s.

Abraham Lincoln called for, and the federal government enacted, the National Homestead Act of 1862. It granted 160 acres of public land to any head of a family 21 years of age or older who agreed to reside upon the land and cultivate it for five years. About 720,000 homesteads were established under the law, and homesteads continued to be available in some states until the early 1900s.

The 1880s and '90s were a time of extreme inequality. A tiny percentage had vast wealth and enjoyed a "Gilded Age," while most Americans struggled and many starved. The **Populist and Progressive movements** produced major reforms and enduring benefits. Two books were especially influential, and each sold more than a million copies. (The U.S. population was under 60 million, so today's equivalent would be six million copies. Each also sold more than a million copies in other countries.) The authors were **Henry George** and **Edward Bellamy.**

Progress and Poverty (1879) by journalist and political economist **Henry George**, sought to explain why poverty persists or increases as societies become wealthier. The main reason, he concluded, is that a few individuals own or control the land. "There is a fundamental and irreconcilable difference between property in things which are the product of labor and property in land." Society can end poverty, he asserted, by abolishing all taxes on income, spending, buildings, and production, and replacing them with a single tax on land.

When Martin Luther King Jr. called for guaranteed income, he quoted *Progress and Poverty*:

> The fact is that the work which improves the condition of mankind, the work which extends knowledge and increases power and enriches literature, and elevates thought, is not done to secure a living. ... It is the work of men who perform it for their own sake, and not that they may get more to eat or drink, or wear, or display. In a state of society where want is abolished, work of this sort could be enormously increased.

George published *The Land Question* in 1881, and called for taxes that confiscate all profits from speculation on land. When speculators profit, the gains are mainly due to public investments in roads, schools, transit, and such, along with population growth, so the profits should be returned to the community:

> There would be at once a large surplus over and above what are now considered the legitimate expenses of government. We could divide this, if we wanted to, among the whole community, share and share alike.

In 1886, he ran for mayor of New York City as an independent, and nearly won. Supporters claimed, and historians concur, that the election was stolen by the Democrats and their infamous Tammany Hall political machine. The Republican who finished third was Theodore Roosevelt, the future U.S. president.

Modern Georgists extend his ideas to include everything people take from nature: oil, coal, gold, timber, minerals, etc., as well as electromagnetic spectrum and the consequences of pollution. Polluters are degrading our common property – air, water, and land that ought to be pristine – so they should compensate us for our losses.

In an 1888 novel, *Looking Backward, 2000-1887,* journalist **Edward Bellamy** imagined an ideal future where all Americans were patriotic and motivated to do what's best for society. Everyone had food, shelter, education, and health care, and everyone between the ages of twenty-one and forty-five had a job. As one character explained, "The worker is not a citizen because he works, but works because he is a citizen." Men and women had opportunities to display their skills and rise to higher levels. All women had a full year of maternity leave with every child. People retired at age forty-five and enjoyed real security for the rest of their lives.

He envisioned a great increase in civility, creativity, and happiness, and an end to crime and social problems. Readers were inspired and motivated. Around the United States, people formed more than 127 "Bellamy clubs" to discuss his ideas and seek ways to implement them.

Early 20th Century England

Bertrand Russell was a philosopher, mathematician, and humanitarian activist. At the end of World War I, in 1918, he published *Proposed Roads to Freedom: Socialism, Anarchism and Syndicalism*:

> The plan we are advocating amounts essentially to this: that a certain small income, sufficient for necessaries, should be secured to all, whether they work or not, and that a larger income – as much larger as might be warranted by the total amount of commodities produced – should be given to those who are willing to engage in some work which the community recognizes as useful. ... When education is finished, no one should be compelled to work, and those who choose not to work should receive a bare livelihood and be left completely free.

He was awarded the Nobel Prize in Literature in 1950.

C.H. "Major" Douglas, a Scottish engineer and economist, analyzed many big companies and concluded that conventional concepts of money are flawed, and the flaws are a major factor in business failures. His books included *Economic Democracy* (1920), *Credit Power and Democracy* (1920), and *Social Credit* (1924).

Credit is a public good, he asserted, and access to credit ought to be a right. He proposed a National Credit Account based on all factors of production and consumption, and a **National Dividend** to provide "absolute economic security." This system, he asserted, will produce "democratic capitalism."

The Social Credit movement spread around the world, with electoral successes in England, Canada, Australia, and New Zealand.

The 1930s

The political pressure to enact **Social Security** came from two national mass movements for guaranteed income, the **Townsend Plan** and **Share Our Wealth.** Both are acknowledged on the Social Security Administration website.

In 1933, the depth of the Great Depression, **Francis Townsend,** a 65-year old family physician in Long Beach, CA, wrote a letter to the editor of his local newspaper, and then expanded it into a short pamphlet, the *Old Age Revolving Pension.*

The **Townsend Plan** sought "Liberal financial retirement for the aged with national recovery and permanent prosperity." Everyone aged 60 or older would get $200 a month (adjusted for inflation, roughly $3,500), with three conditions: recipients had to obey the law, quit any paid work, and spend the money. That spending would create jobs for younger workers, thereby ending the Depression and bringing "permanent prosperity" for society. To fund the plan, Townsend proposed a 2 percent sales tax on all business transactions.

Over the following year, roughly 2.2 million people joined Townsend Clubs, and they actively supported candidates in the 1934 election. Congress invited Townsend to appear and present his ideas, and he did that in February 1935. President Franklin Roosevelt signed the Social Security law on August 14, 1935.

But the payments were much smaller than Townsend sought, and he denounced the program.

Share Our Wealth called for $2,500 a year for every family (about $44,000 today), funded through taxes on the very rich. They claimed to have 7.7 million members in 1935, with groups in every state. The founder and leader, **Huey Long,** a U.S. Senator and former governor of Louisiana, was planning to run for president against incumbent Franklin Roosevelt. But in September 1935, Long was assassinated by the son of a political rival.

Historians often describe Long as a "demagogue" or "populist," using those labels to disparage him and his campaign. But the facts remain: his followers had valid grievances and meaningful demands.

In 1935, British economist and professor at Oxford University **George D. H. Cole** proposed a **social dividend**. All production involves public assets and our common heritage, he reasoned, so all citizens ought to share the profits. **James Meade,** also at Oxford, endorsed the social dividend as a central element in a just society. Meade was awarded the Nobel Memorial Prize in Economics in 1977.

American economist **Abba Lerner** expressed support in 1936. Polish economist **Oskar Lange** proposed a modified version in 1937. Both were on the faculty of the London School of Economics.

The 1940s and '50s

Franklin Roosevelt spoke about "Four Freedoms" in his State of the Union address on January 6, 1941. That was more than a year after World War II began in Europe, and eleven months before the United States entered the fighting. The four freedoms he identified were:

> Freedom of speech and expression ... freedom of every person to worship God in his own way ... freedom from want — which, translated into world terms, means economic understandings

which will secure to every nation a healthy peacetime life for its inhabitants — everywhere in the world ... [and] freedom from fear ...

"Freedom from want" may be unattainable without basic income. With it, moreover, the other freedoms may be inevitable.

Three years later, in his State of the Union on January 11, 1944, and in a fireside chat to the American people the same evening, he proposed "a second Bill of Rights."

We have come to a clear realization of the fact that true individual freedom cannot exist without economic security and independence. ... People who are hungry and out of a job are the stuff of which dictatorships are made. ... In our day these economic truths have become accepted as self-evident. We have accepted, so to speak, a second Bill of Rights under which a new basis of security and prosperity can be established for all — regardless of station, race, or creed.

His proposed economic rights included a job with a living wage, a decent home, medical care, education, and recreation.

Economist and social theorist **Friedrich Hayek** was acclaimed as an opponent of socialism and a champion of free markets. In *The Road to Serfdom* (1944), the most popular of his many books, he condemned government programs because they encroach on markets and constrain people's freedom and security. Yet he endorsed the goal of providing "the security of a minimum income." He wrote:

There can be no doubt that some minimum of food, shelter, and clothing, sufficient to preserve health and the capacity to work, can be assured to everybody. ... [This is] no privilege but a legitimate object of desire ... [that] can be provided for all outside of and supplementary to the market system.

He shared the Nobel prize in economics in 1974. Four years later, in *Legislation and Liberty,* he restated his support for basic economic security:

> The assurance of a certain minimum income for everyone, or a sort of floor below which nobody need fall even when he is unable to provide for himself, appears not only to be wholly legitimate protection against a risk common to all, but a necessary part of the Great Society in which the individual no longer has specific claims on the members of the particular small groups into which he was born.

The Great Transformation: the Political and Economic Origins of Our Time (1944), by economic historian **Karl Polanyi,** examined labor, land, and money, and the immense changes that occurred with the industrial revolution in the late 1700s. People were taking jobs in factories, in many cases after being forced off the land, and there was a brutal increase in poverty. In 1795, justices from the region around Speenhamland, England, met

> ... in a time of great distress, [and] decided that subsidies in aid of wages should be granted in accordance with a scale dependent upon the price of bread, so that a minimum income should be assured to the poor *irrespective of their earnings.*

Speenhamland "introduced no less a social and economic innovation than the 'right to live.'" Workers, families, and society benefitted, and "it became the law of the land over most of the countryside." The subsidy program lasted for nearly 40 years, despite serious flaws and mounting problems, until it was replaced with the New Poor Law of 1834.

Markets are "embedded" in society, Polanyi showed, neither superior nor separate. Markets express political choices. The modern ideal is a self-regulating free market, but that requires ongoing political support. When societies allow or expect markets to self-regulate, personal freedom and democracy are diminished.

His ideas remain relevant, even prescient. We're living through a digital revolution and a great disruption, with many parallels to the industrial revolution. His book is a compelling argument for basic income.

The first person to propose a **negative income tax** was British writer and politician **Juliet Rhys-Williams,** in 1944.

American economist **George Stigler** endorsed it in 1946. He was on the faculty of the University of Chicago, with Milton Friedman, and a founding member of the Mont Pelerin Society with Friedman and Friedrich Hayek. Stigler was awarded the Nobel in economics in 1982.

Eleanor Roosevelt was world-renowned as an advocate for social justice, and in 1948 the newly-formed United Nations invited her to lead a commission on human rights and freedom. Their efforts produced the **Universal Declaration of Human Rights.** The General Assembly adopted it on December 10, 1948, with only eight countries abstaining and none voting against it. Today, the **UDHR** is widely cited and respected around the world, and many countries have elements of it in their constitutions. Two items in particular:

> Article 3: Everyone has the right to life, liberty and security of person.
>
> Article 25: Everyone has the right to a standard of living adequate for the health and well-being of himself and of his family, including food, clothing, housing and medical care and necessary social services, and the right to security in the event of unemployment, sickness, disability, widowhood, old age or other lack of livelihood in circumstances beyond his control.

In *The New Society* (1949), **Peter Drucker,** a pioneer in business management theory and practice, proposed a **predictable income** to "banish the uncertainty, the dread of the unknown and the deep feelings of insecurity under which the worker today lives." The predictable income would be minimal, and could be varied when economic conditions change.

Guaranteed income, he stated, is fundamentally different from any effort to guarantee jobs or wages. A job or wage guarantee "would not be worth the paper on which it is written. It would give the worker the illusion of security which is bound to be cruelly disappointed" during economic downturns. Such practices could also "freeze the economy ... subsidizing obsolescent industries and restricting, if not stopping, technological progress."

The term **basic income** was first used in 1953 by British economist **George D. H. Cole.**

John Kenneth Galbraith, an economist at Harvard University, published *The Affluent Society* in 1958 and it was a bestseller. Familiar ideas are often flawed, he stated, and he urged readers to confront the "conventional wisdom" (a phrase he coined, intended as irony). In a chapter on "The Divorce of Production from Security," he questioned common assumptions about jobs:

> The answer is to find some way of diminishing the reliance now being placed on production as a source of income. ... to provide alternative sources of income, unrelated to production, to those whom the modern economy employs only with exceptional difficulty or unwisdom.

In 1966, after serving as an advisor to President John F. Kennedy, Galbraith wrote an essay on "The Starvation of the Cities."

We need to consider the one prompt and effective solution for poverty, which is to provide everyone with a minimum income. The arguments against this proposal are numerous, but most of them are excuses for not thinking about a solution, even one that is so exceedingly plausible.

Idleness, we agree, is demoralizing. But even here there is a question: Why is leisure so uniformly bad for the poor and so uniformly good for the exceptionally well-to-do? ... We can easily afford an income floor. ... And there is no antidote for poverty that is quite so certain in its effects as the provision of income.

He revised *The Affluent Society* in 1969, and added a few sentences:

For those who are unemployable, employable only with difficulty, or who should not be working, the immediate solution is a source of income unrelated to production. This has come extensively into discussion under various proposals for a guaranteed income or a negative income tax. The principle common to these proposals is provision of a basic income as a matter of general right.

(He also added a footnote: "A discussion that has developed since the earlier editions of this book. I did not then think such ideas within the realm of practical political feasibility.")

"The Unfinished Business of the Century," a 1999 paper presented at the London School of Economics, focused on two concerns with "high visibility and urgency. The first is the very large number of the very poor even in the richest countries and notably in the United States."

The answer or part of the answer is rather clear: everybody should be guaranteed a decent basic income. A rich country such as the United States can well afford to keep everybody out of poverty. Some, it will be said, will seize upon the income and won't work. So it is now with more limited welfare, as it is called. ... Let us accept some resort to leisure by the poor as well as by the rich.

His second major concern was the need to eliminate nuclear weapons. "The most urgent task now and of the new century is to bring to an end the threat of Armageddon."

The 1960s

In *The Challenge of Abundance* (1961), socio-economist and futurist **Robert Theobald** examined automation and social trends. "Many changes will be necessary as we move from an economy of scarcity to an economy of abundance." We must establish "new principles specifically designed to break the link between jobs and income."

He expanded on these ideas in *Free Men and Free Markets* (1963), with a specific proposal:

> The need is clear: the principle of an economic floor under each individual must be established. This principle would apply equally to every member of society and carry with it no connotation of personal inadequacy or implication that an undeserving income was being received from an overgenerous government. ...
>
> Basic Economic Security can be best regarded as an extension of the present Social Security system to a world in which conventional job availability will steadily decline. ...
>
> *We will need to adopt the concept of an absolute constitutional right to an income. This would guarantee to every citizen of the United States ... the right to an income from the federal government sufficient to enable him to live with dignity.*

Basic Economic Security, his term, "would be very simple to operate compared to the present mosaic of measures ... which have been introduced at various times in the past to meet the same goal." He called for cutting other programs to pay for the guaranteed income.

Capitalism and Freedom was first published in 1962. In a chapter on the alleviation of poverty, economist **Milton Friedman** asserted that "the arrangement that recommends itself on purely mechanical grounds is a negative income tax."

> The advantages of this arrangement are clear. It is directed specifically at the problem of poverty. It gives help in the form most useful to the individual, namely, cash. It is general and could be substituted for the host of special measures now in effect. It makes explicit the cost borne by society. It operates outside the market.

Friedman advised Barry Goldwater in his 1964 campaign for president, served on Richard Nixon's committee of economic advisors, and was awarded the Nobel in economics in 1976. In *Free to Choose* (1980), a book and PBS television series written with his wife Rose, he stated that:

> We should replace the ragbag of specific welfare programs with a single comprehensive program of income supplements in cash — a negative income tax. It would provide an assured minimum to all persons in need, regardless of the reasons for their need, while doing as little harm as possible to their character, their independence, or their incentives to better their own conditions. ... A negative income tax provides comprehensive reform which would do more efficiently and humanely what our present welfare system does so inefficiently and inhumanely.

In his first State of the Union Address, on January 8, 1964, **Lyndon Johnson** declared an "unconditional war on poverty in America."

> Our chief weapons in a more pinpointed attack will be better schools, and better health, and better homes, and better training, and better job opportunities to help more Americans, especially young Americans, escape from squalor and misery and unemployment rolls where other citizens help to carry them.

Along with action on poverty and civil rights, he called on Congress to enact "the most far-reaching tax cut of our time." And he pledged to make government "efficient, and honest and frugal," with "an actual reduction in Federal expenditures and Federal employment" that would "cut our deficit in half."

The War on Poverty was a partial victory. During his administration, the poverty rate fell from 22 percent to 13 percent. The rate has rarely been lower since then, and only briefly. (In September 2016, the U.S. Census Bureau announced a rate of 13.5 percent, 1.2 percent lower than a year before, though it's still 43.1 million people who are officially defined as poor.)

Johnson initiated three substantial steps toward guaranteed income. He appointed a **National Commission on Technology, Automation, and Economic Progress** and a **National Commission on Income Maintenance Programs.** And he created the Office of Economic Opportunity, which funded and managed a series of **Income Maintenance Experiments** around the country.

In the spring of 1964, 35 leading thinkers and political activists, the **Ad-Hoc Committee on the Triple Revolution,** published a 14-page report about three interrelated developments: "cybernation," their term for computers and automation; weaponry, particularly nuclear weapons; and the universal demand for full human rights. "Gaining control of our future requires the conscious formation of the society we wish to have."

They presented a number of proposals, starting with:

> We urge, therefore, that society ... undertake an unqualified commitment to provide every individual and every family with an adequate income as a matter of right. ... The unqualified right to an income would take the place of the patchwork of

welfare measures. ... the distribution of abundance in a cyber-
nated society must be based on criteria strikingly different from
those of an economic system based on scarcity.

The committee was sponsored by the Center for the Study of
Democratic Institutions in Santa Barbara, CA. One member was
Linus Pauling, recipient of the 1962 Nobel Peace Prize (after a 1954
Nobel in Chemistry; only one other person, Marie Curie, has received
Nobel prizes in two different fields). Another was Gunnar Myrdal,
who subsequently shared the 1974 Nobel prize in economics. Robert
Theobald was also a member. Their final paragraph:

Democracy, as we use the term, means a community of men and
women who are able to understand, express, and determine
their lives as dignified human beings. Democracy can only be
rooted in a political and economic order in which wealth is distributed by and for people, and used for the widest social benefit. With the emergence of the era of abundance, we have the
economic base for a true democracy of participation, in which
men no longer need to feel themselves prisoners of social forces
and decisions beyond their control or comprehension.

The Triple Revolution report influenced Martin Luther King Jr.
and was featured in an award-winning 1967 science fiction novella,
"Riders of the Purple Wage," by Philip José Farmer.

The Guaranteed Income: Next Step in Economic Evolution?
(1966), edited by Robert Theobald, presented papers by ten eminent
social scientists. **Erich Fromm,** a pioneer in humanistic psychology,
wrote about "The Psychological Aspects of the Guaranteed Income."

The principle prevailing throughout most of human history in
the past and present is: "He who does not work shall not eat."
This threat forced man not only to act in accordance with what

was demanded of him but also to think and to feel in such a way that he would not even be tempted to act differently.

Guaranteed income would not only establish freedom as a reality rather than a slogan, it would also establish a principle deeply rooted in Western religious and humanist tradition: man has the right to live, regardless! This right to live, to have food, shelter, medical care, education, etc., is an intrinsic human right that cannot be restricted by any condition, not even the one that he must be socially 'useful.'

The shift from a psychology of scarcity to that of abundance is one of the most important steps in human development. ... Liberation from fear of starvation would mark the transition from a prehuman to a truly human society.

Aside from the fact that there is already no work for an ever increasing sector of the population, and hence that the question of incentive for these people is irrelevant. ... It can be demonstrated that material incentive is by no means the only incentive for work and effort. First of all there are other incentives: pride, social recognition, pleasure in work itself, etc. Secondly, it is a fact that man, by nature, is not lazy, but on the contrary suffers from the results of inactivity. People might prefer not to work for one or two months, but the vast majority would beg to work, even if they were not paid for it.

Another contributor was **Marshall McLuhan,** widely-known for his ideas about the social impacts of technology and mass communication. His paper was "Guaranteed Income in the Electric Age."

Guaranteed income must increasingly include the satisfaction we gain from effective involvement in meaningful work. "Leisure," which the artist always enjoys, is created by the fullest possible employment of the faculties in creative activity. ... The guaranteed income that results from automation could therefore be understood to include that quite unquantifiable factor of joy and satisfaction that results from a free and full disclosure of one's powers in any task organized to permit such activity.

Technology and the American Economy was a 1966 report from the **National Commission on Technology, Automation, and Economic Progress,** created by President Lyndon Johnson. One conclusion:

> Technological change and productivity are primary sources of our unprecedented wealth, but many persons have not shared in that abundance. We recommend that economic security be guaranteed by a floor under family income. That floor should include both improvements in wage-related benefits and a broader system of income maintenance for those families unable to provide for themselves.

Commission members were presidents of major corporations, presidents of labor unions, and prominent academics. They included Daniel Bell (chairman, Sociology Department, Columbia University); Patrick E. Haggerty (president, Texas Instruments); Edwin H. Land (president, Polaroid Corporation); Walter P. Reuther (president, United Automobile Workers); Robert M. Solow (professor of economics, MIT, and a 1987 Nobel laureate); and Thomas J. Watson, Jr. (chairman of the board, IBM Corporation).

Martin Luther King Jr. called for a guaranteed income in his final book, *Where Do We Go From Here: Chaos or Community?* (1967). "Up to recently we have proceeded from a premise that poverty is a consequence of multiple evils." The proposed remedies are piecemeal, insufficient, uncoordinated, and "have another common failing — they are indirect. Each seeks to solve poverty by first solving something else." He continued:

> I am now convinced that the simplest approach will prove to be the most effective — the solution to poverty is to abolish it directly by a now widely discussed measure: the guaranteed income. ... We are likely to find that the problems of housing

and education, instead of preceding the elimination of poverty, will themselves be affected if poverty is first abolished.

Idleness and unemployment are serious concerns, he acknowledged, though often follow market dislocations, leaving many people trapped against their will. With guaranteed income, everyone will have opportunities to pursue meaningful and fulfilling work. He quoted from *Progress and Poverty* by Henry George, and cited John Kenneth Galbraith to show that guaranteed income is affordable.

Personal dignity is vital for social justice, King suggested:

> A host of positive psychological changes inevitably will result from widespread economic security. The dignity of the individual will flourish when the decisions concerning his life are in his hands, when he has the assurance that his income is stable and certain, and when he knows that he has the means to seek self-improvement.
>
> There is nothing except shortsightedness to prevent us from guaranteeing an annual minimum – and livable – income for every American family.

Guaranteed income "is not a 'civil rights' program, in the sense that term is currently used," because all of the poor will benefit, and two-thirds of the poor are white.

> If democracy is to have breadth of meaning, it is necessary to adjust this inequity. It is not only moral, but it is also intelligent. We are wasting and degrading human life by clinging to archaic thinking.
>
> The curse of poverty has no justification in our age. ... The time has come for us to civilize ourselves by the total, direct and immediate abolition of poverty.

Every January, on the holiday that commemorates King's life, we hear bits of his 1963 "I Have a Dream" speech and his 1964 Nobel Peace Prize acceptance, but rarely anything from the years that followed. Yet *Where do We Go From Here* is still relevant, and the final passages are most eloquent:

> In a real sense, all life is interrelated. The agony of the poor impoverishes the rich; the betterment of the poor enriches the rich. ... Whatever affects one directly, affects all indirectly.
>
> A true revolution of values will soon cause us to question the fairness and justice of many of our past and present policies. ... A true revolution of values will soon look uneasily on the glaring contrast of poverty and wealth. ... America, the richest and most powerful nation in the world, can well lead the world in this revolution of values.
>
> These are revolutionary times. ... We are confronted with the fierce urgency of *now*.

In the spring of 1968, **Paul Samuelson**, the 1970 Nobel laureate in economics, and four other prominent economists – **John Kenneth Galbraith**, **Robert Lampman**, **Harold Watts**, and **James Tobin**, who was awarded the Nobel in 1981 – published a letter calling on Congress "to adopt this year a national system of income guarantees and supplements." They wrote:

> Like all civilized nations in the twentieth century, this country has long recognized a public responsibility for the living standards of its citizens. Yet our present programs of public assistance and social insurance exclude the millions who are in need and meet inadequately the needs of millions more.
>
> As economists we offer the professional opinion that income guarantees and supplements are feasible and compatible with our economic system. As citizens we feel strongly that the time for action is now.

Their letter was widely circulated among their colleagues, with an invitation to sign. Over the following months, more than 1,200 economists signed it.

Cultural anthropologist **Margaret Mead** was a prominent author and a regular contributor to *Redbook,* a popular magazine that mainly markets to married women. She discussed guaranteed income in a column in the spring of 1968.

> The danger that we would be underwriting the failures is trivial compared with the benefits the guaranteed annual income would provide us. It would provide dignity for every citizen and choice for every citizen.

Philip Wogaman, a minister and professor of Christian social ethics, published *Guaranteed Annual Income: The Moral Issues* in 1968. His conclusion, after examining various concerns, disputes, and objections: "The case for guaranteed income is persuasive on both ethical and practical grounds." He wrote:

> Man's right to be – his right to physical and social existence – is not something for his fellowmen to grant or withhold as an economic inducement or give as a gift. ...
>
> Guaranteed income as a secure economic floor will make it possible for men to become what God intended them to become by free response. The fact that many will doubtless abuse this freedom is a risk which God has taken in creating man in the first place. ... [T]his right to be is one which God has given to each of us regardless of our undeserving. Guaranteed income will be a recognition, in economic terms, of what God has done.

He also stated that "Christians may have some unique contribution to make with respect to the guaranteed income issue." And with their passion for justice, they "may have a duty to endorse guaranteed income."

His appendix includes statements in support of guaranteed income from the National Council of Churches of Christ in the U.S.A., the United Methodist Church, and a special committee of the United Presbyterian Church in the U.S.A.

R. Buckminster Fuller was an architect, futurist, and design scientist. In *Operating Manual for Spaceship Earth* (1969), he wrote:

> Our labor world and all salaried workers ... are now at least subconsciously if not consciously, afraid that automation will take away their jobs. They are afraid they won't be able to do what is called "earning a living," which is short for earning the right to live. The term implies that normally we are supposed to die prematurely and that it is abnormal to be able to earn a living.
>
> [W]e must give each human who is or becomes unemployed a life fellowship in research and development or in just simple thinking. Man must be able to dare to think truthfully and to act accordingly without fear of losing his franchise to live.
>
> Through the universal research and development fellowships, we're going to start emancipating humanity from being muscle and reflex machines. We're going to give everybody a chance to develop their most powerful mental and intuitive faculties.

On August 8, 1969, seven months after taking office, **President Richard Nixon** gave a televised address on poverty and welfare:

> We face an urban crisis, a social crisis — and at the same time, a crisis of confidence in the capacity of government to do its job. ... Nowhere has the failure of government been more apparent than in its efforts to help the poor and especially the system of public welfare.
>
> That is why tonight I therefore propose that we abolish the present welfare system and that we adopt in its place a new family assistance system. Initially, this new system will cost more than welfare. But unlike welfare, it is designed to correct the condition it deals with and thus to lessen the long-range burden and cost.

For a family of four now on welfare, with no outside income, the basic Federal payment would be $1,600 a year. States could add to that amount and most states would add to it. In no case would anyone's present level of benefits be lowered.

This new system establishes a direct link between the government's willingness to help the needy and the willingness of the needy to help themselves. It removes the present incentive not to work and substitutes an incentive to work; it removes the present incentive for families to break apart and substitutes an incentive for families to stay together. It removes the blatant inequities, injustices, and indignities of the welfare system. It establishes a basic Federal floor so that children in any state have at least the minimum essentials of life.

Nixon's **Family Assistance Plan** was a guaranteed income or negative income tax, according to it's author, **Daniel Patrick Moynihan**, although Nixon didn't use either term. (In a 1973 book, cited below, Moynihan quoted Nixon's speechwriter, William Safire, who said the talk was crafted "to make a radical proposal seem conservative.")

That November, after 22 months of hearings around the country, the **National Commission on Income Maintenance Programs** published its report. Appointed by President Lyndon Johnson, the chairman was Ben W. Heineman (president of Northwest Industries). Members included Thomas J. Watson Jr. (chairman of IBM); David Sullivan (president of the Service Employees International Union); civil rights leader A. Philip Randolph; politicians Edmund G. Brown and Barbara Jordan; and economist Robert Solow (who was awarded the Nobel prize in 1987). The executive director was Robert A. Harris.

Their unanimous report, *Poverty Amid Plenty: the American Paradox,* called for "a new program of income supplementation for all Americans in need."

Our main recommendation is for the creation of a universal income supplement program financed and administered by the Federal Government, making cash payments to all members of the population with income needs. The payments would provide a base income for any needy family or individual.

Work requirements ... cannot be used effectively in determining eligibility for aid, and are undesirable in any case. ... Inevitably, any simple test designed to withhold aid from the voluntarily unemployed will deal harshly with some of those who cannot find work.

Our observations have convinced us that the poor are not unlike the non-poor. Most of the poor want to work. They want to improve their potential and to be trained for better jobs. Like most Americans, the poor would like to do something with their lives beyond merely subsisting. By providing them with a basic system of income support, we provide them with an opportunity to do these things.

We do not believe that work disincentive effects of the proposed program would be serious.

The 1970s

Nixon's **Family Assistance Plan** had widespread support, according to public opinion polls, and major newspapers endorsed it. On April 16, 1970, the House of Representatives passed it with a margin of nearly two-to one.

In the Senate Finance Committee, extreme liberals wanted more generous assistance, while extreme conservatives opposed any increased aid to the poor. The committee delayed until after the election in November. Then the extremists on both sides voted against it — and defeated the moderates. The full Senate never considered it.

The new Congress convened in January 1971, and a slightly revised version was introduced as H.R. 1, which normally indicates a high priority bill. The House passed it again by two-to-one. And the Senate blocked it again.

The plan's author was Nixon's principal domestic policy advisor, **Daniel Patrick Moynihan,** who later served as a Democratic senator from New York. In *The Politics of a Guaranteed Income: the Nixon administration and the Family Assistance Plan* (1973), he described in detail how the plan was conceived, presented, debated, and defeated. He blamed the defeat on several factors: Nixon's refusal to spend any political capital; the skillful maneuvering of conservative opponents in the Senate; the timidity of liberals in the Senate, combined with the ambitions of those who wanted to use the issue in their 1972 campaigns; and the misguided, shortsighted actions of the National Welfare Rights Organization, which demanded more generous benefits and organized against it.

Another factor in that defeat was the release of preliminary data from the **Income Maintenance Experiments,** which were conducted by the federal Office of Economic Opportunity. The experiments began in 1967 as part of Lyndon Johnson's War on Poverty, continued until 1974, and included 8,500 people in New Jersey, Denver, Seattle, and elsewhere, in urban, suburban, and rural communities. Poor families received guaranteed cash payments. Researchers tracked recipients' incomes, work hours, family situations, and other variables.

During the Senate Finance Committee debates about the Family Assistance Plan, in 1970, senators demanded the preliminary partial data. The data showed a decline in total work hours. Opponents cited the decline as a reason to reject the plan. Proponents had no response; even Moynihan, the plan's author, was dispirited.

The final results showed a decline in total work hours of 6 percent to 13 percent. Yet that was mainly among women and teens: wives chose to stay home with their kids, teens stayed in school or went back to school. There were also men who left bad jobs and were out of work temporarily. People were pursuing their dreams and goals, and their actions were good for society. In other words, that decline was a healthy sign.

Because the experiments were politicized and publicized before they were analyzed, the results are often mischaracterized. Even today, some people cite the preliminary data, whether inadvertently or intentionally, and use it as a reason to oppose basic income. (Another preliminary "result" was a higher divorce rate, but that was a statistical anomaly; there was no sign of it in the final analyses.)

In 2002, the State University of New York at Stony Brook sponsored a conference that featured a panel of scholars who worked on the design, implementation, and evaluation of the experiments. They stated emphatically, unanimously, that the experiments clearly indicated the potential benefits of basic income.

That panel discussion is presented in "A Retrospective on the Negative Income Tax Experiments: Looking Back at the Most Innovative Field Studies in Social Policy" (2005) by Karl Widerquist, et al. Another noteworthy article (though quite academic) is "A Failure to Communicate: what (if anything) can we learn from the negative income tax experiments?" (2005) by Karl Widerquist. Both articles are at https://works.bepress.com/widerquist/.

"A national guaranteed income" was in the original 1970 platform of the **D.C. Statehood Party,** the first political party in the world to endorse this idea. The party is still active as the **D.C. Statehood Green Party.**

George McGovern was a U.S. Senator from South Dakota and the Democratic candidate for President in 1972. During that campaign, he called for universal **Demogrants** — guaranteed payments of $1,000 a year for every American, including children. (About $5,000 today). The payments were to be phased-out or taxed-back from people with higher incomes.

The proposal was written by **James Tobin**, who was a member of President John F. Kennedy's Council of Economic Advisors from 1961 to 1962. It never received a fair hearing, and Tobin subsequently stated that McGovern "botched" the initial presentation. Tobin was awarded the Nobel in economics in 1981.

When Congress debated Nixon's Family Assistance Plan, the main advocate was **Gerald Ford,** the Republican leader in the House of Representatives. He promoted it forcefully, resisted conservative objections, and succeeded twice in winning two-thirds of the vote. Ford became president in the summer of 1974, after Nixon resigned. A year later, Ford endorsed and signed a scaled-back version, the **Earned Income Tax Credit,** which provides money only to low-wage workers, and does nothing for the unemployed.

The **EITC** is truly bipartisan, with widespread support in Congress. Ronald Reagan proposed and signed a major expansion, and there have also been increases under George H.W. Bush, Bill Clinton, George W. Bush, and Barack Obama. More than 30 million workers benefit and, at $82 billion a year, it's now America's largest welfare program. Most states and several local governments have their own programs that supplement the federal payment.

In July 1975, the **National Urban League,** under executive director **Vernon E. Jordan Jr.**, called for a **Universal Refundable**

Credit Income Tax, a reformed welfare system that sought to place a floor under all incomes. They identified five goals or principle characteristics:

I. The system should be adequate, equitable, and universal.
II. The system should be federally administered and funded.
III. The benefits should not be work conditioned.
IV. Benefits should be cash rather than in kind.
V. The goal of the new program should be income maintenance.

During the debates about Nixon's Family Assistance Plan, then-governor of Georgia **Jimmy Carter** was the only southern governor who endorsed it. While running for president in 1976, he called for comprehensive welfare reform. Two years later, President Carter presented his **Program for Better Jobs and Income Support**. His party, the Democrats, controlled both houses of Congress, but the plan never got a full hearing because the party was deeply divided and Carter was personally unpopular.

The 1980s

Businessman and aviation inventor **Leonard M. Greene** published *Free Enterprise Without Poverty: A Bold Plan, Full-fledged Capitalism with Economic Security for All* in 1981. He called for a **National Tax Rebate,** "a simple, universal cash grant of $1,000 a month for every American family of four." The funds were to come from cutting government programs.

He subsequently set out to test the plan. As described in *The National Tax Rebate: a New America with Less Government* (1998), his Institute for SocioEconomic Studies ran ads in newspapers and on radio shows throughout the country, asking people to

Tell us what you'd do with an extra $1,000 a month; and would you trade government benefits for a monthly check? To encourage individuals and families to respond, the institute broadcast that it would select three families from all those who wrote back, and award them a demonstration tax rebate of $1,000 a month for twenty years.

Thousands of people responded. His book describes the three selected families, with photos, and reports on how they were using the money. Although the project was supposed to last twenty years, the payments were stopped at some point. Greene died in 2006.

Alaska has a small basic income, the **Permanent Fund Dividend.** It began in 1982 under **Jay Hammond**, a Republican who was governor from 1974 to 1982.

Oil was discovered in Alaska in 1969, and the state constitution was amended to create the **Alaska Permanent Fund.** A percentage of oil royalties goes into the Fund, which invests in a diverse portfolio for the benefit of current residents and future generations; that's what makes it permanent. Dividends are paid each year to everyone who resides in the state for more than six months of the year, including children. The amount varies with oil prices, interest rates, investment markets, and other factors, and is normally between $1,000 and $2,000.

In 2016, the **PFD** was $1,022. The 2015 dividend was a record, $2,072 (which is $8,288 for a family of four).

The previous peak was 2008, when it was $2,069, and that year people also got a one-time bonus, an extra $1,200, so the total for a family of four was $13,076. The governor at the time was Sarah Palin. She championed that bonus, and it was a major reason for her high approval ratings at the time — and therefore a significant factor in John McCain's selecting her to run for vice president. During their presidential campaign, though, they didn't talk about the PFD and journalists didn't ask.

Alaskans love the PFD, and have rejected several attempts to curtail it. Research shows that people use the money to pay debts, send kids to college, and save for retirement. Income inequality in Alaska is the lowest of the 50 states, and that's mainly – perhaps entirely – due to the PFD.

Perhaps they'll expand it: PFD Plus. Funds can come from higher oil royalties, taxes on other takings, reallocated money from the federal government, and a reinstated income tax. (Alaska eliminated it's income tax when it created the Permanent Fund. After he retired, Gov. Hammond said that had been a mistake, and called for restoring it.)

Two books of articles about the PFD are *Alaska's Permanent Fund Dividend: Examining its Suitability as a Model* (2012) and *Exploring the Alaska Model: Adapting the Permanent Fund Dividend for Reform around the World* (2012). Both were edited by basic income proponents Karl Widerquist and Michael Howard.

Allan Sheahen, an independent scholar-activist, published *Guaranteed Income: the Right to Economic Security* in 1983. He rewrote it thirty years later as *Basic Income Guarantee: Your Right to Economic Security* (2013).

At a 1986 meeting in Belgium, a group of economists, sociologists, political scientists, and philosophers founded the **Basic Income European Network.** Through publications and biannual congresses, the idea spread and the network grew. The 2002 **BIEN** congress was in Geneva, and attracted participants from around the world. At the final session, Brazilian Senator **Eduardo Matarazzo Suplicy** proposed that the group redefine the 'E' — and BIEN became the **Basic Income Earth Network.**

BIEN welcomes everyone who's interested in these ideas, and does not endorse any particular version or proposal. Their formal definition of a basic income (as revised in 2016) emphasizes five core features: periodic, cash, individual, universal, unconditional:

> A basic income is a periodic cash payment unconditionally delivered to all on an individual basis, without means-test or work requirement.

For the Common Good: Redirecting the Economy toward Community, the Environment, and a Sustainable Future (1989, and a 1994 second edition) is by economist **Herman E. Daly**, then at Louisiana State University and subsequently at the World Bank, and process theologian **John B. Cobb** of Claremont College.

They called for a negative income tax as one way to further the ideals in their subtitle. And they strongly endorsed Henry George's proposal to shift property taxes off buildings and onto the full rental value of land.

The 1990s

In 1990, scholar-activists **Jeffrey J. Smith** and **Gary Flomenhoft** founded the **Geonomy Society** to advance the ideas of Henry George plus **Citizen's Dividends.** "Geonomy" or "geoism" emphasizes the fact that all economic activity – all life, in fact – starts with the earth.

Philippe Van Parijs, philosopher, political economist, and founding member of **BIEN**, is the author or editor of several books, including *Arguing for Basic Income: Ethical Foundations for a Radical*

Reform (1992) and *Real Freedom for All: What (if Anything) can Justify Capitalism?* (1997).

What's Wrong with a Free Lunch (2001) features a paper by Van Parijs, with responses from a number of eminent social scientists, including **Gar Alperovitz**, **Emma Rothschild**, and **Herbert Simon**, a 1978 Nobel laureate in economics. The forward is by economist **Robert Solow**, who served on the President's Commission on Income Maintenance and received the Nobel in 1987.

Van Parijs also published a 2017 book with **Yannick Vanderborght**, *Basic Income: a Radical Proposal for a Free Society and a Sane Economy.*

Another **BIEN** co-founder is economist **Guy Standing**. He published several papers on basic income in the '90s, and currently teaches at the University of London. He was the main organizer of the 2002 BIEN Congress, which was held at the headquarters of the International Labor Organization in Geneva, and he edited a book of papers from that Congress, *Promoting Income Security as a Right, Europe and North America* (2005).

Standing is also the author of *The Precariat: the New Dangerous Class* (2011), and *A Precariat Charter: from Denizens to Citizens* (2014). Both books analyze the social dislocation and disengagement that's happening worldwide, and call for basic income as a necessary solution. He was the lead economist in the pilot projects in Namibia and India, and is a co-author, with Sarath Davala and others, of *Basic Income: a Transformative Policy for India* (2015). In 2017, he published *The Corruption of Capitalism: Why Rentiers Thrive and Work Does Not Pay.*

A former welfare mother in New York City, and a political activist, **Theresa Funiciello** published *Tyranny of Kindness: Dismantling the Welfare System to End Poverty in America* in 1992. After describing the abuses, indignities, disincentives, and inefficiencies in the welfare system, she concluded that guaranteed income is the only viable solution.

James Robertson, a British scholar, activist, and author, and a co-founder of the New Economics Foundation, has for several decades been calling for a **Citizen's Income**. In a September 1992 newsletter, he discussed fundamental flaws with conventional policies:

> More and more people realise that full employment is a thing of the past. But politicians continue to argue that their party's policies will eventually bring it back. A costly job creation industry continues to flourish at the taxpayer's expense, but to little effect. And the rules continue to create an "unemployment trap" and a "poverty trap" which stop people building up work for themselves. ...
>
> The longer the present arrangements go on, the more people's lives will be spoiled and wasted, and the more damaging the resulting social alienation and unrest will be. A priority for the next few years must be a campaign to liberate work from employment.

His insights and warnings are still valid. American politicians in both major parties are obsessed with efforts to create jobs. "Social alienation and unrest" are now epidemic.

The End of Work: the Decline of the Global Labor Force and the Dawn of the Post-Market Era (1995) is by **Jeremy Rifkin,** a professor at the Wharton School and a leading analyst of economic trends. Examining the huge productivity gains – and the huge loss of jobs, and the harm to workers – brought by robots, computers, the internet, and related technologies, he concluded:

> Every country must ultimately grapple with an elementary question of economic justice. ... Since the advances in technology are going to mean fewer and fewer jobs in the market economy, the only effective way to ensure those permanently displaced by machinery share the benefits of increased productivity is to provide some kind of government-guaranteed income. ... With guaranteed income independent of their jobs, workers would be more free to set their own schedules and adapt to changing conditions. That adaptability would in turn allow greater flexibility for employers, plus many benefits for society as a whole.

David Korten has a Ph.D. from Stanford Business School, was a captain in the U.S. Air Force during the Vietnam war, and taught at Harvard Business School. With that conservative establishment background, he then worked for decades in international business and public policy. He published *When Corporations Rule the World* in 1995, with a second edition in 2001.

The book begins by reviewing common assumptions about poverty, equity, development, and economic growth, and then presents a history of corporate power in the United States. His conclusion: corporations are inherently harmful. In a chapter on "Agenda for Change," he presents a number of remedies, including guaranteed income. Assessing the impact on work incentives and labor markets, he wrote:

> Since earned income would not reduce the guaranteed payment, there would be little disincentive to work for pay, though employers might have to pay more to attract workers to unpleasant, menial tasks. If some choose not to work, this should not be a considered a problem in a labor surplus world.

Other agenda items include various ways to fund the guaranteed income, such as a financial transactions tax, a surtax on short-term capital gains, and shifting taxes onto resource extraction and other environmentally-harmful activities. His larger goals are "localizing the global system" and building a movement for "a living democracy."

Hazel Henderson, futurist, evolutionary economist, and founder of Ethical Markets Media, is a long-time supporter of a guaranteed income or negative income tax. She considered these ideas in several places, including *Building a Win-Win World* (1996).

The $30,000 Solution: a Guaranteed Annual Income for Every American, (1996) is by **Robert Schutz,** who was a lecturer in economics and business administration at the University of California Berkeley. His calculation of $30,000 for every adult was based on redistribution of all unearned income: rent, interest, capital gains, dividends, winnings, gifts, and inheritance.

The **Eastern Band of Cherokee Indians** in North Carolina opened a casino in 1997, and began distributing some of the profits directly to all tribal members, including children. (Money for children goes into a bank account until they graduate high school or reach age 21.) Everyone gets about $4,000 a year, with a payment every six months.

Several years prior to that, researchers from Duke University initiated a study of children's mental health in western North Carolina. They randomly selected 1,420 children, and the group included 350 American Indians. One of the researchers, **Jane Costello,** a professor of medical psychology at Duke, has described their research as an experiment on basic income — and uniquely significant because they started the study before the tribe began distributing money.

Four years after the casino opened, Indian children had fewer behavioral and emotional problems than did neighboring children. Moreover, the effect continued into adulthood. At age 30, one in five of the American Indians had mental health or drug problems, compared with one in three of those in surrounding communities. The Indians had less depression, anxiety and alcohol dependence. ... The younger the participants were when their families started getting the casino payments, the stronger the effects on adult mental health.

Addressing concerns about people spending the money on drink or drugs, Costello noted that non-Indians also drink, take drugs, and waste money. "Most people used their income supplement wisely ... and there was no evidence that people worked fewer hours." With more than 20 years of evidence, the research "strongly suggests that on the whole, universal basic income works."

Her 2016 article, http://www.salon.com/2016/06/21/many_countries_are_weighing_cash_payments_to_citizens_could_it_work_in_the_u_s/.

Charles M. A. Clark is a professor of economics at Fordham University and a past president of the Association for Evolutionary Economics. His books include *Pathways to a Basic Income* (1997, with John Healy); *Basic Income: Economic Security for all Canadians* (1999, with Sally Lerner and Robert Needham); *The Basic Income Guarantee: Ensuring Progress and Prosperity in the 21st Century* (2002); and *Rediscovering Abundance*, (2006, with Helen Alford, Steve Cortright, and Mike Naughton).

He was a co-founder of the U.S. Basic Income Guarantee Network (USBIG) in 1999.

Michael L. Murray is the author of *And Economic Justice for All: Welfare Reform for the 21st Century* (1997). A retired professor of insurance at Drake University in Iowa, he sought a guaranteed adequate income combined with a flat income tax, and showed in detail that this would be affordable.

"How to make society civil and democracy strong" is the subject and subtitle of *A Place for Us* (1998) by social theorist **Benjamin R. Barber**. In the final chapter he states:

> We have to find new ways to distribute the fruits of nonlabor-based productivity to the general population, *whether or not they work for their living*. Otherwise, more and more citizens will become poor in economic and social terms ... [and the system itself] will be undermined and destroyed by political instability, new forms of class war, and – most ironic of all – by not enough income-earning consumers to buy all the goods in this labor-free world.

The sooner we act, he suggests, the greater the gains. "Once the political will is in place to decouple work and reward, many feasible innovations are possible."

In 1998, independent scholar-activist **Steven Shafarman** published his first book about guaranteed income, *Healing Americans: a New Vision for Politics, Economics, and Pursuing Happiness.* Over the following decade he wrote three more books, *Healing Politics: Citizen Policies and the Pursuit of Happiness* (2000); *We the People: Healing our Democracy and Saving our World* (2001); and *Peaceful, Positive Revolution: Economic Security for Every American* (2008).

Bruce Ackerman and Anne Alstott are professors at Yale University Law School and authors of *The Stakeholder Society* (1999). "As each American reaches maturity, he or she will be guaranteed a stake of

$80,000." Through stakeholding, they argue, "Americans can win a renewed sense that they do indeed live in a land of equal opportunity where all have gotten a fair chance." As an alternative, they endorse:

[A]n unconditional cash payment each year to each adult. Everyone would get the basic income, regardless of their other income or wealth. ... We urge its serious consideration in the United States. Like stakeholding, the basic income puts the emphasis on freedom. With a basic income, everyone could count on at least four thousand dollars a year. The sum hardly opens up a life of leisure, but it would grant most Americans greater freedom to shape their lives.

Like stakeholding, the basic income grants this freedom and security without strings attached. It automatically supplements low wages without bureaucracy or complex wage subsidies. And with a basic income, more people can choose for themselves whether to work full-time or part-time, making their own tradeoffs between more money and more leisure.

They also co-wrote a book with Philippe Van Parijs, *Redesigning Distribution: Basic Income and Stakeholder Grants as Cornerstones for an Egalitarian Capitalism* (2006).

The **U.S. Basic Income Guarantee Network** was founded in December 1999 by Karl Widerquist, Michael Lewis, Fred Block, Charles M. A. Clark, and Pam Donavan, social scientists at various universities. Other long-time leading members include Eri Noguchi, Almaz Zelleke, and Michael Howard. The first **USBIG** conference was in New York City in March 2002, sponsored by the State University of NY at Stony Brook. Yearly meetings have followed, co-sponsored in recent years by Basic Income Canada and sometimes held in Canada.

From 2000 through mid-2017

When George W. Bush took office in 2001, the federal budget had large surpluses, though the U.S. economy was in a recession from the bursting of a stock market bubble. The **Congressional Progressive Caucus** – Representatives Bernie Sanders, Barbara Lee, Dennis Kucinich, and 50 other Democrats and independents – called for an **American People's Dividend:** $300 to every citizen, including children. Sponsors wanted the dividend to be repeated yearly if surpluses continued, as expected. Their proposal was endorsed by the AFL-CIO and other groups.

That dividend was in the first tax cut bill passed in the House of Representatives, which at the time was controlled by the Democrats. Republicans opposed it, however, and the Senate bill scaled it back. The conference committee compromised on a one-time distribution of $300 to people who pay income taxes, with nothing for children, and nothing for poor folks who have no income or incomes too low to be taxed. President Bush signed the law on June 7, 2001.

In July, every taxpayer got a check for $300, or $600 for couples who filed jointly. That distribution was a major factor in quickly ending the recession.

A week or so before mailing the checks, the Bush administration sent a letter to every taxpayer, claiming credit for the direct payments. The Progressive Caucus' role was erased.

Sociocenomic Democracy: An Advanced Socioeconomic System (2002) is by **Robley E. George,** the founder of the Center for the Study of Democratic Society. He examines current economic models, including capitalism, socialism, communism, and mixed economies, and demonstrates that all have serious flaws. His proposed alternative, "socioeconomic democracy," combines a universal guaranteed income and maximum allowable personal wealth, and he asserts that both are necessary for any true democracy.

Marshall Brain created *How Stuff Works* and teaches entrepreneurship at the University of North Carolina. In *Manna*, a 2003 novel, he proposed a guaranteed basic income of $25,000 for every U.S. citizen. This would simultaneously (1) "create the largest possible pool of consumers," (2) promote "maximum economic stability," (3) "create the largest possible pool of innovators," (4) encourage investment, and (5) provide people with "maximum freedom."

In June 2004, the **Green Party of the United States** adopted a platform plank calling for a universal "livable income." Green parties around the world support basic income as a pillar in their call for social and economic justice.

Karl Widerquist is an economist and a professor of philosophy at Georgetown University–Qatar, and was a co-founder of USBIG. He has written or edited several books about basic income, including *The Ethics and Economics of the Basic Income Guarantee* (2005); *Alaska's Permanent Fund Dividend: Examining its Suitability as a Model* (2012); and *Exporting the Alaska Model: Adapting the Permanent Fund Dividend for Reform Around the World* (2012).

Charles Murray is a resident scholar at the American Enterprise Institute and author of several influential books, including *In Our Hands: a Plan to Replace the Welfare State* (2006, and a second edition in 2016). His plan would provide $10,000 a year to everyone age 21 and over, plus $3,000 for mandatory health insurance.

To fund it, he wants to eliminate all federal, state, and local programs that transfer funds to individuals or favored groups. His 2016 appendix lists the federal programs, with dollar amounts from 2014, along with ideas about state and local transfers. He calculates total savings of $2.77 trillion — more than enough money to pay for his plan. (More about his plan is in Appendix 2.)

Stanley Aronowitz, a prolific author, long-time labor organizer, and professor at City University of New York Graduate Center, has endorsed a guaranteed basic income in several books, including *Left Turn: Forging a New Political Future* (2006).

The **Tax Cut for the Rest of Us Act of 2006,** H.R. 5257, would have created a small basic income by transforming the standard tax deduction into a "fully refundable" tax credit of $2,000 for each adult and $1,000 for each child. Everyone who filed a tax form, even if they had no income, would have received that amount. **Allan Sheahen** and **Karl Widerquist** conceived the idea. The sponsor was **Representative Bob Filner** from San Diego. It was never debated.

The Earth Belongs to Everyone (2008), by **Alanna Hartzok,** is a collection of articles and essays from her decades of work as scholar, educator, and activist for the ideas of Henry George. She also highlights Thomas Paine's *Agrarian Justice,* particularly his idea that the earth is the "common heritage of mankind." Modern Georgists, including Hartzok, sometimes describe basic income as a "**common heritage dividend.**"

Joseph V. Kennedy is an economist and attorney with experience in the public and private sectors, and was Chief Economist of the U.S.

Department of Commerce under George W. Bush. In *Ending Poverty: Changing Behavior, Guaranteeing Income, and Transforming Government (2008),* he proposes:

> A bilateral, annual, and voluntary contract between the government and any citizen above the age of twenty-one who wishes to participate. The government would hopefully guarantee the individual a minimum income of at least $20,000.

We Hold These Truths: the Hope of Monetary Reform (2008) is by **Richard C. Cook,** who was a government analyst for 32 years, mostly at the U.S. Treasury Department and with NASA. An admirer of C.H. Douglas and the Social Credit movement, Cook is most concerned with flaws in America's monetary system. In the 19th century, the federal government would simply issue money and spend it into circulation. That's how the Lincoln administration funded northern forces in the Civil War, with "Greenbacks." When the Federal Reserve was created in 1913, Cook asserts, the real motives were to fund wars and to boost the economic and political power of the finance industry.

He wants to "abolish the Federal Reserve as a bank of issue," authorize "credit to be directly issued by the U.S. Treasury," and "issue an annual guaranteed basic income to all legal U.S. residents."

Barack Obama was elected president in the early months of the Great Recession, the worst economic decline since the Great Depression of the 1930s. His stimulus plan, the **American Recovery and Reinvestment Act of 2009,** included a change in withholding for Social Security. Every worker got a payroll tax credit – extra money in our paychecks – of up to $2,200 a year. The credit continued for several years.

People spent the money, demanding goods and services. That spending was a significant factor in the recovery.

When they designed the stimulus, the Obama administration was concerned that people might save that money or mainly use it to pay debts. To promote spending and economic growth, they deliberately downplayed the payroll tax credit, while emphasizing other features, especially government spending on "shovel-ready" projects. In other words: Obama created a universal tax credit, but didn't flaunt it. He gave people money, yet avoided acclaim. Has any other politician ever done that?

Capital in the 21st Century by **Thomas Piketty** was a bestseller in 2014. Income inequality was a major concern at the time, thanks mainly to Occupy Wall Street and its offshoots. Piketty, a professor at the Paris School of Economics, used historic data that provided new insights into inequality and why and how it persists. Inequality increases faster than economic growth, he showed, and therefore government must intervene. He calls for wealth taxes to fund government assistance for poor and working class folks.

He also endorses basic income. He discusses it in *The Economics of Inequality* (1997 French edition, translated in 2015), and in recent articles and interviews.

In *With Liberty and Dividends for All: How to Save our Middle Class when Jobs Don't Pay Enough,* (2014) journalist and businessman **Peter Barnes** endorses a basic income funded through taxes on natural wealth, carbon taxes in particular. With these combined policies, he maintains, we can achieve rapid progress on slowing global warming and reducing income inequality.

Robert B. Reich was Secretary of Labor under Bill Clinton, and co-creator and star of the 2013 film *Inequality for All*. He's now on the faculty of the University of California Berkeley. *Saving Capitalism: for the Many, not the Few* (2015) examines fundamental flaws in our political and economic system. "A Citizen's Bequest," his next-to-last chapter, endorses a "basic minimum income," with a brief history of related ideas. He's reaffirmed his support in several blog posts and short videos.

People Get Ready: the Fight Against a Jobless Economy and Citizenless Democracy (2016) is by **Robert W. McChesney**, a professor at the University of Illinois at Urbana-Champaign, and **John Nichols,** a columnist for *The Nation.* Their main focus is the massive disruptions we're experiencing with changing technologies. Their last chapter, "A Democratic Agenda for a Digital Age," considers what we must do to move forward:

> If we may generalize, the one solution that has currency, and that is promoted by scholars who have done so much to identify concerns outlined in this book, is the notion of a basic income or guaranteed annual income for all people in the nation.

But it might be "a phony solution." Society has to invest in education. "Why not make it the national policy that *every* child in America gets the same caliber of education as the children of the wealthy?" We must also "democratize the Constitution," "democratize journalism," "democratize planning," and "democratize the economy."

Andy Stern is a former president of SEIU, the Service Employees International Union, and was appointed by President Obama to the National Commission on Fiscal Responsibility and Reform (known as Simpson-Bowles). He's currently on the faculty at Columbia

University. With **Lee Kravitz,** he wrote *Raising the Floor: How a Universal Basic Income Can Renew Our Economy and Rebuild the American Dream* (2016). Their version is "$1,000 per month for all adults between the age of eighteen and sixty-four and for all seniors who do not receive at least $1,000 per month in Social Security payments."

Stern is especially attentive to financial matters. The total cost of his plan would be "between $1.75 trillion and $2.5 trillion per year in government spending." He presents a range of options for raising the funds. (More about his plan is in Appendix 2.)

Utopia for Realists: How We Can Build the Ideal World (2017, first published in Dutch in 2014) is by journalist and independent scholar **Rutger Bregman.** His main theme is the title of chapter 2: "Why We Should Give Free Money to Everyone." Among the many reasons, he discusses the experiment in Dauphin, Canada; the research with the Eastern Cherokee in North Carolina; and ongoing projects in Kenya and Uganda.

"How do we make utopia *real*? How do we take these ideas and implement them?" A vital step, he suggests:

> Everyone who reckons themselves progressives should be a beacon of not just energy but ideas, not only indignation but hope, and equal parts ethics and hard sell. ... the most vital ingredient for political change: the conviction that there truly is a better way. That utopia really is within reach.

Venture investors and technology innovators are expressing support — and providing funds for pilot projects and educational programs:

- **Sam Altman** of Y Combinator, a major start-up incubator in Silicon Valley, announced plans to fund a basic income experiment with 100 poor families in Oakland, CA.
- *World After Capital* is an online book-in-progress by **Al Wenger**, managing partner of Union Square Ventures, a venture capital firm.
- **GiveDirectly**, a nonprofit based in New York City, is "working with leading economists to organize an ambitious experiment that will rigorously test the impact of different models of basic income over 12 years in Kenya."
- Facebook co-founder **Chris Hughes** launched the **Economic Security Project** "to support exploration and experimentation with unconditional cash stipends."

Barack Obama also acknowledged the potential. "Whether a universal income is the right model — that's a debate that we'll be having."

Note: This history omits items that are highly academic or mainly summarize cited sources. It also omits material primarily from and about other countries.

* * * * *

This chronological history conveys a compelling story with a core theme, overlapping narratives, and continuing drama.

The Founders were concerned about economic security, and similar concerns may have been broadly popular at the time. Mass movements emerged in the 1880s and '90s (the Populists and Progressives); in the 1930s (the Townsend Plan and Share Our Wealth); and the 1960s, when economic issues were intertwined with campaigns for civil rights, women's rights, and the mobilization to end the war in Vietnam.

Each uprising was ignited by public distress about poverty and inequality. Each brought real progress and lasting reforms, though far less than the activists sought. Each was followed by a few decades of relative quiet. The closest we've come to enacting a version of basic income was in the early 1970s, with serious policy debates and government-funded experiments — but without a mass movement, the opportunity was missed.

The quiet time is ending. Over the last few years, especially in early 2017, public interest is growing rapidly. There are now myriad blogs, Facebook pages, YouTube videos, and TEDx talks. Activists in the United States are fortified by related efforts around the world. We are starting to mobilize an irresistible mass movement.

We will have a basic income.

The questions now are when? And how?

The answers are up to us.

Appendix 2:

Financial Matters

Potential allies are often deterred by doubts about finances: How will we pay for it? Where will the money come from? Will it increase budget deficits? What about the national debt?

The answers are actually straightforward. Financial matters really are secondary. Our government will find the funds when We the People force our demands.

Moreover, if folks are sincerely concerned about balancing the federal budget and paying down the national debt, this plan is imperative. These goals are unattainable with current policies and politics.

Recall the recession of 2008 and 2009. After the housing bubble burst, and banks and brokers went bankrupt – and millions of Americans lost homes, jobs, and retirement savings – Congress gave Wall Street an $800 billion bailout. Then the Federal Reserve created $4.1 trillion and gave that to Wall Street. Politicians also "saved" the auto industry with $80 billion. Earlier in that decade, our government authorized spending for the wars in Afghanistan and Iraq, now at least $1.6 trillion, possibly $6 trillion. Bailouts for Wall Street and the auto industry; huge sums for foreign wars; and with routine matters, too — government creates money, and spends it, before collecting taxes or other revenues.*

Our national government can readily create the funds. At $500 or $1,000 a month, the total will be one to two trillion dollars a year, far less than it gave to Wall Street. Americans will be financially secure and united, unlike today. Everyone will have means and incentives to work together – We the People – to defeat special interests, cut or eliminate programs, reform the tax code, rescind regulations, and so on. Cuts and reforms can begin immediately.

Two recent books include budget numbers. *In Our Hands: A Plan to Replace the Welfare State* is by Charles Murray (a 2016 update from a first edition in 2006). *Raising the Floor: How a Universal Basic Income can Renew our Economy and Rebuild the American Dream,* also 2016, is by Andy Stern and Lee Kravitz. Their analyses are especially significant because they have opposite political orientations. Murray is a scholar at the American Enterprise Institute and a self-proclaimed libertarian, though some call him a conservative. Stern, an avowed progressive, was president of a major labor union, SEIU (Service Employees International Union). He was also on the National Commission on Fiscal Responsibility and Reform (Simpson-Bowles), appointed by President Obama.

Murray's plan is $10,000 a year for everyone age 21 and over, plus $3,000 for mandatory health insurance. To fund it, he wants to eliminate all federal, state, and local programs that transfer funds

---

*Government creates money all the time, though most of us, including basic income proponents, overlook that fact. One way to understand the process is to view government as a bank. When a bank issues a loan, it has only a small fraction on hand, a few percent, and it creates the rest with a bookkeeping entry. Borrowers repay their loans, ideally, plus interest.

We'll repay our government by spending our Citizen Dividends, thereby producing jobs, economic growth, and tax revenues. We'll also pay interest by actively working to shrink and reform our government.

to individuals or favored groups. He lists the federal programs in an appendix, with dollar amounts from 2014. He writes:

> The bulk of the money to finance a UBI would come from just three programs of transfers to individuals: Social Security (which includes disability payments as well as pensions), Medicare, and Medicaid. All are unambiguously transfers and they are huge. In 2014, outlays to pay them amounted to 72 percent of federal transfers to individuals.

His appendix also discusses cuts in state and local transfers. He calculates a total of $2.77 trillion — more than enough money to pay for his plan.

Stern is seeking "$1,000 per month for all adults between the age of eighteen and sixty-four and for all seniors who do not receive at least $1,000 per month in Social Security payments." The total cost would be "between $1.75 trillion and $2.5 trillion per year in government spending." His proposed funding options:

- cutting 126 welfare programs, for a total of $1 trillion a year.
- eliminating expenditures through the tax code – credits, deductions, exemptions, and subsidies – for $1.2 trillion a year.
- introducing a value added tax of 5 to 10 percent on the consumption of goods and services, an estimated $650 billion to $1.3 trillion.
- implementing a small financial transaction tax, $150 billion.
- charging corporations for the use or taking of public assets, including air, water, data, and electromagnetic spectrum.
- levying a small wealth tax on "the total value of personal assets" beyond $1 million.
- cutting government spending — the military budget, farm subsidies, subsidies to oil and gas companies, and so on.

Stern and Murray are not alone. Many economists and policy analysts have looked at the numbers and agree: there's more than enough money available.

This book takes funding suggestions from Stern and Murray and other proponents, plus a wide range of additional possibilities for savings and gains. Let's put everything on the table, consider our options, seek consensus, and compromise. After we enact any version of this plan, everyone will have incentives to work together toward deeper cuts and additional reforms.

We can positively afford a basic income. We cannot afford current policies and practices.

Financial matters are compelling reasons to act now.

Appendix 3:
International Activities

Canada conducted several income maintenance experiments in the 1970s. One was a "saturation site" in Dauphin, Manitoba, a rural town of 10,000. Nearly 1,000 residents received unconditional monthly payments from 1974-1979. But the program was stopped after political changes in the province and the national government, and the files were stored without compiling the results.

Decades later, health economist Evelyn Forget, a professor at the University of Manitoba, located the Dauphin data and devoted several years to analyzing it. She found significant health improvements, plus a steep decrease in poverty, higher employment, and improved education outcomes.

An article about Forget and Dauphin, headlined "A Canadian City Once Eliminated Poverty and Nearly Everyone Forgot About It," appeared in the Huffington Post in 2014. http://www.huffingtonpost. ca/2014/12/23/mincome-in-dauphin-manitoba_n_6335682.html.

Public radio's *Marketplace* did a story in 2016. https://www. marketplace.org/2016/12/20/world/dauphin.

Canada's national government and several provinces are launching pilot projects in 2017.

Mexico, conditional cash transfers: Mexico began providing cash to poor residents in 1997, initially to help people who were harmed by NAFTA (the North America Free Trade Agreement). They expanded the program in 2002, and renamed it. *Oportunidades* has been remarkably successful, and in the poorest states it now helps nearly half of all families. One sign that it works: Mexicans have been leaving the United States and going home, a net outflow over recent years. (Immigrants across the southern border are mainly coming from Honduras, Guatemala, and El Salvador, after traveling through Mexico.)

Just Give Money to the Poor: The Development Revolution from the Global South (2010) is by Joseph Hanlon, Armando Barrientos, and David Hulme, academics with extensive experience studying international development. They present a comprehensive review of the research with cash transfer programs in Mexico, Brazil, Columbia, Peru, and other countries. People use the money responsibly. Participants benefit significantly, in health, education, and employment. Poverty declines and tax revenues increase.

Cash transfers are an efficient and effective way to reduce poverty, and are now policy in more than 50 countries, including China and India. A 2014 World Bank article discusses Mexico's program (now called *Prospera*) and how it has been a model for the world. http://www.worldbank.org/en/news/feature/2014/11/19/un-modelo-de-mexico-para-el-mundo.

Brazil started giving money to the poor in 2001, a conditional program to keep kids in school. They expanded it in 2003 into the *Bolsa Familia* (Family Grant). On the tenth anniversary, the World Bank published an opinion article that summarized the gains:

> [Bolsa Familia] has been key to help Brazil more than halve its extreme poverty – from 9.7 to 4.3 % of the population. Most impressively, and in contrast to other countries, income inequality also fell markedly. ... Equally important, qualitative

studies have highlighted how the regular cash transfers from the program have helped promote the dignity and autonomy of the poor. This is particularly true for women, who account for over 90% of the beneficiaries.

The ultimate goal of any welfare program is for its success to render it redundant. Brazil is well placed to sustain the achievements over the last decade and is close to reaching the amazing feat of eradicating poverty and hunger for all Brazilians, a true reason to celebrate. http://www.worldbank.org/en/news/opinion/2013/11/04/bolsa-familia-Brazil-quiet-revolution.

More than 60 million Brazilians were getting monthly payments in 2016. That's 30 percent of the population of 200 million.

Brazilians now have a legal right to a minimum income. Their Senate passed that unanimously, and President Luiz Inácio Lula da Silva signed it in January 2004. The sponsor, Senator Eduardo Matarazzo Suplicy, learned about guaranteed income when he lived in the United States in the late 1960s, while earning his Ph.D. in economics.

The 2003 debate about rebuilding Iraq: On April 9, 2003, three weeks after the U.S. invasion, the New York Times published an op-ed proposing an Alaska-style fund for the Iraqi people. The author was Steven C. Clemons, executive vice president of New America, a prominent think tank.

Most revolutions that produce stable democracies expand the number of stakeholders in the nation's economy. ... Iraq's annual oil revenue comes to approximately $20 billion. A postwar government could invest $12 billion a year in infrastructure to rebuild the nation. The other $8 billion could anchor an Iraq Permanent Fund. ... The resulting income would go directly to Iraq's six million households.

Establishing this fund would show a skeptical world that America will make sure Iraq's oil revenues directly benefit Iraqi citizens. By spreading capital broadly among new stakeholders, the plan would also prevent a sliver of Iraq's elite from becoming a new kleptocracy. Finally, the creation of an Iraqi oil fund could begin to help repair America's damaged image abroad — itself no small dividend at a time when many people remain suspicious about American motives in the Middle East. http://www.nytimes.com/2003/04/09/opinion/sharing-alaska-style.html.

Secretary of State Colin Powell testified before Congress in favor of the idea, and said the Bush administration was considering it.

Senators Lisa Murkowski, a Republican from Alaska, and Mary Landrieu, a Democrat from Louisiana, introduced a Senate resolution in support of an "Iraqi Freedom Fund."

New York Times columnist John Tierney wrote about the possibility on September 10, 2003:

The notion of diverting oil wealth directly to citizens, perhaps through annual payments like Alaska's, has become that political rarity: a wonky idea with mass appeal, from the laborers in Tayeran Square to Iraq's leaders. ... The concept is also popular with some Kurdish politicians in the north and Shiite Muslim politicians in the south, who have complained for decades of being shortchanged by politicians in Baghdad. http://www.nytimes.com/2003/09/10/world/struggle-for-iraq-iraq-s-wealth-popular-idea-give-oil-money-people-rather-than.html.

But it never happened. (Unconfirmed reports are that Vice President Dick Cheney killed it.)

Namibia: In late 2007 through 2009, 930 residents of Otjivero-Omitara, a poor rural village, received monthly payments of 100 Namibian dollars (equal to about U.S.$12). The project was privately funded, with contributions from people in Germany, England, the

United States, and elsewhere. As summarized by Spanish economist Daniel Raventos, the payments:

> reduced poverty from 76% to 16%; child malnutrition fell from 42% to 10%; school dropout rates plummeted from 40% to almost 0%; average family debt dropped by 36%; local police reported that delinquency figures were 42% lower; and the number of small businesses increased, as did the purchasing power of the inhabitants, thereby creating a market for new products. http://www.counterpunch.org/2015/08/21/the-basic-income-debate-political-philosophical-and-economic-issues/.

A 2009 feature in the German magazine *Der Spiegel* described it as "A New Approach to Aid: How a Basic Income Program Saved a Namibian Village." http://www.spiegel.de/international/world/a-new-approach-to-aid-how-a-basic-income-program-saved-a-namibian-village-a-642310.html.

According to opinion polls, Namibians want a national program. Elected officials are also on record in support. But Namibia is a poor country, so a national program would require outside funding.

India: In a project organized by SEWA, the Self-Employed Women's Association of India, in 2011-2013, eight poor rural villages were randomly chosen from a group of twenty. (The other twelve were used as a comparison group.) Every resident received a monthly grant. Adults got 200 rupees (equal to about U.S.$3.50), with 100 rupees for children. (The money for children was paid to the mother.) After the first year, the amounts increased to 300 and 150 rupees. About 6,000 people received payments. The project was funded by UNICEF (United Nations Children's Fund) India.

As reported in the French journal, *Le Monde Diplomatique*:

Studies at the beginning, mid-point, and end of the project confirmed that, in villages receiving payments, people spent more on eggs, meat, and fish, and on healthcare. Children's school marks improved in 68% of families, and the time they spent at school nearly tripled. Saving also tripled, and twice as many people were able to start a new business. http://mondediplo.com/2013/05/04income.

Recipients worked more hours than people in the comparison villages. There was no increase in alcohol consumption. Perhaps most significant, recipients continued to benefit even after the payments stopped — with better sanitation, more education, new businesses, and, especially among women, greater personal dignity.

SEWA also organized an urban pilot project in Delhi. There, too, the outcomes were extremely positive.

Basic Income: A Transformative Policy for India (2015) is by Sarath Davala, Renana Jhabvala, Guy Standing, and Soumya Kapoor Mehta, the organizers and researchers.

Foreign Affairs published "Why India is Ready for a Universal Basic Income: How it Could Cut Poverty and Bureaucracy" in April 2017. https://www.foreignaffairs.com/articles/india/2017-04-06/why-india-ready-universal-basic-income.

Kenya, Uganda, and Rwanda: Nonprofit organizations in Europe and the United States have funded small pilot projects that had successful outcomes. In these countries and others, funds can be deposited and transferred using cell phones; the projects were partly designed to test that system, and it proved to be efficient, effective, and empowering.

Eight, based in Belgium, announced in 2016 that they're launching a two year project in Uganda and planning to make a documentary film. http://eight.world/.

GiveDirectly, a New York group with several years experience in Kenya and Rwanda, is now "working with leading economists to organize an ambitious experiment that will rigorously test the impact of different models of basic income over 12 years in Kenya." They're raising $30 million, and in mid 2017 they already had most of that amount. https://www.givedirectly.org/.

The New York Times Magazine had a long story. https://www.nytimes.com/2017/02/23/magazine/universal-income-global-inequality.html.

A Vox article included more background on basic income. https://www.vox.com/policy-and-politics/2017/3/6/14007230/kenya-basic-income-givedirectly-experiment-village.

European countries: In October 2013, Swiss activists submitted signatures for a national referendum. To mark the occasion and attract more supporters, organizers dumped eight million 5-cent coins, one for each Swiss citizen, in the plaza outside the Federal Palace in Bern. They then invited people to play, picnic, or stay overnight on the coins. The event was widely reported in the United States and around the world. They also created the world's largest poster (as certified by Guinness World Records): "What would you do if your income were taken care of?"

From the start, the Swiss activists expected to win only on a second round. The referendum was on June 5, 2016, and was defeated. In the next round, thanks in part to their efforts, they'll be able to cite results from nearby pilot projects. Several countries might already have national programs. The past campaign and future plans are at www.basicincome2016.org.

Also in 2013, proponents throughout the continent were promoting a European Citizens' Initiative for Unconditional Basic Income. Although they didn't manage to qualify under the rules of the European Union, they attracted, educated, and organized allies in many countries. Their campaign generated a new organization, Unconditional Basic Income Europe (UBIE). http://basicincomeeurope.org.

Finland, Holland, Italy, Scotland, and other countries are launching pilot projects in 2017 (in specific cities, though mostly funded by national governments).

* * * * *

The pilot project we need now is a whole country. Who wants to be first?

Canada, Finland, Holland, Italy, etc., are wealthy democracies. The projects they're conducting or launching are almost certain to prove the efficacy of basic income. If citizens decide to move forward, they can readily afford to implement national programs.

Mexico, Brazil, and other countries could extend their programs and remove the conditions. They might have true, though small, basic incomes within a few years.

Namibia, India, Kenya, and Uganda are relatively or extremely poor. They and similar countries may be eager to volunteer — if outside funds are available.

Activists in wealthy countries can press our governments to fund poor countries' programs, redirecting foreign aid, perhaps increasing aid. We can also call for support from the World Bank, International Monetary Fund, United Nations, and other transnational agencies.

Philanthropists might offer funds. Countless foundations have charters that mandate spending on health, education, sanitation, poverty reduction, women's rights, and other goals that are sure to gain with this approach. Several foundations are large enough to single-handedly fund a small country for a year or two or longer.

Citizens of small countries might design programs and publish requests for funds. (A meaningful pilot could also be a state or region within a country.) Some points to consider:

- What would be an appropriate basic income?
- How much funding would be required for one year? For two years?
- How will finds be distributed? Cash? Bank accounts? Cell phone transfers?
- Which current programs could be cut or eliminated?
- What about reforming the tax code and financial system?
- How is this likely to affect health, education, justice, and so on?
- How will the program be evaluated? When? By whom?
- What will happen if, or after, outside funding ends?

For donors, this will be an investment, not a handout. A basic income pilot project will probably cost less than current aid programs (though only after high start-up and transition costs). Recipient countries will become more self-sufficient.

With any pilot project, news will quickly spread to nearby countries and around the world. Within a few months or a year, residents of neighboring countries are likely to demand their own basic income programs. Projects might be in or near regions that are currently afflicted with wars, refugees, terrorism, famines, or droughts. Those countries and regions will be more secure and prosperous. Our world will be more peaceful.

Appendix 4:

For More Information

Basic Income Action is a nonprofit organization with local groups around the United States. Their mission is to win a basic income for all by educating and organizing people to take action. www.basic incomeaction.org.

The **Basic Income Earth Network** was founded in 1986, initially as the Basic Income European Network. The **BIEN** website has links to many national and transnational organizations, plus regular news updates from around the world. www.basicincome.org.

Unconditional Basic Income Europe connects activists from more than 25 countries. The organization formed as a follow-up to a 2013 campaign that gathered nearly 300,000 signatures for a European Citizens' Initiative for Unconditional Basic Income. http://basic income-europe.org.

The **U.S. Basic Income Guarantee Network** started in 1999 as an informal association of academics and activists. USBIG hosted its first annual conference in 2002, in New York City, with yearly conferences since then, in recent years combined with Basic Income Canada. The website has an extensive collection of discussion papers and other materials. www.usbig.net

www.basicincomeimperative.com is the website for this book, with a blog, updates, and links to political campaigns.

Notes

1. Chapter 1, page 5. Note the comma and dash in "... the pursuit of happiness, — that to secure these rights ... ." A period is standard, sometimes with the dash, but the period appears to be a mistake, an error by the first newspaper to print the Declaration. This is a recent discovery, though it can't be confirmed because the handwritten versions are too faded. The National Archives in Washington D.C. examined it in a June 2015 forum with Danielle Allen, a professor of government at Harvard University, and other scholars. She initiated the inquiry with her 2014 book, *Our Declaration: a Reading of the Declaration of Independence in Defense of Equality.* My punctuation is the version she prefers.

(The original texts, handwritten and printed, have capital letters in the middle of sentences, and those capitals complicate questions about the comma or period. Punctuation practices were changing at the time. In the Constitution, eleven years later, punctuation and capitalization are mostly like today.)

With a comma, Allen observed, the sentence is a syllogism; a mode of formal logic with a first premise, second premise, and conclusion. The classic example, from Aristotle: All men are mortal; Socrates is a man; therefore, Socrates is mortal. In the Declaration: All men are created equal and have unalienable rights; to secure our rights, governments are instituted by consent; therefore, if government is dysfunctional, instituting new government is a right.

With a period, that logic is lost or obscured. The period separates the opening clauses from the statements that follow. Those clauses get extra emphasis. Readers reach the period, pause to praise these self-evident truths, then often only skim the rest.

The first premise is about individual rights. "We hold these truths to be self-evident, that all men are created equal, that they are endowed by their creator with certain unalienable rights, that among these are life, liberty, and the pursuit of happiness, … "

The second premise proclaims the reciprocity between people and governments. The dash distinguishes it, especially when there's also a dash at the end. "… — that to secure these rights, governments are instituted among men, deriving their just powers from the consent of the governed, — … "

The conclusion combines and extends both premises. The first word is "that," like the second premise and three clauses in the first premise. With a comma, all five "that" statements are self-evident truths. "… that whenever any form of government becomes destructive of these ends, it is the right of the people to alter or to abolish it, and to institute new government, laying its foundations on such principles, and organizing its powers in such form, as to them shall seem most likely to effect their safety and happiness."

More evidence of the original intent: The first premise of the Declaration includes Aristotle's opening words, "all men are." Also, the first premise and the conclusion have the same last word, "happiness," a parallel to Aristotle's "mortal." Furthermore, the premises use similar phrases, "men are created" and "are endowed," and "governments are instituted." The conclusion shifts to active language and proffers guidance about how to institute a new government.

226 BASIC INCOME IMPERATIVE

The complete 110-word sentence is a coherent logical argument, a syllogism, that declares our sovereignty with an elegant, powerful demand for democracy.

Thomas Jefferson wrote the Declaration with assistance from John Adams, Benjamin Franklin, Robert R. Livingston, and Roger Sherman, the drafting committee selected by the Continental Congress. Four were lawyers, and all five would have known Aristotle's syllogism. They also knew theories of government from Locke, Spinoza, Montesquieu, Rousseau, and other Enlightenment thinkers. They worked together for two and a half weeks, and presumably debated every word, comma, colon, semi-colon, and period. Then the full Congress debated the Declaration for several days and made additional changes.

Danielle Allen's preferred punctuation – a comma, plus two dashes to mark the syllogism – might become the new standard. I hope so. I believe this small change can make a big difference in helping Americans recognize our roles, rights, and responsibilities as citizens.

2. Chapter 2, page 14. Basic income, as defined by the Basic Income Earth Network, is "a periodic cash payment unconditionally delivered to all on an individual basis, without means-test or work requirement." Five features: periodic, cash, individual, universal, unconditional.

I'm campaigning for the core concept, and calling for compromise on the details and features. Many versions are for citizens only; others include legal residents. Most are for adults only; some add a smaller amount for children, and a number of proponents call for universal child benefits as a parallel program. Some are not truly universal or are partly conditional.

Proponents have used various names for various theoretical reasons or political purposes. Early terms include *national dividend,* from C.H. Douglas in 1920; *social dividend,* from George D. H. Cole and James Meade in 1935; *negative income tax,* from Juliet Rhys-Williams in 1944; *predictable income,* from Peter Drucker in 1949; and *basic income,* from George D. H. Cole in 1953.

Basic Economic Security is from Robert Theobald in 1963; he also used *guaranteed income.* That was a year after Milton Friedman popularized *negative income tax.* Throughout the 1960s and beyond, *negative income tax* was the preferred term among conservatives, to convey their desire to simplify the tax code and cut government programs. Liberals normally say *guaranteed income,* to emphasize social and economic justice; sometimes *guaranteed annual income, guaranteed adequate income,* or *guaranteed minimum income.*

The *Family Assistance Plan* was a guaranteed income or negative income tax, according to its author, Daniel Patrick Moynihan. He used both terms, though Richard Nixon avoided both when he presented it in 1969. *Demogrants* is from James Tobin, economic policy advisor to George McGovern, Democratic candidate for president in 1972. After Nixon was reelected, defeating McGovern, Democrats and Republicans abandoned these ideas — although both parties support the *Earned Income Tax Credit,* which helps workers only.

Basic income became the common term after 1986, with the founding of the Basic Income Earth Network. Proponents often expand it to *universal basic income, unconditional basic income,* or *UBI.* Or to *basic income grant, basic income guarantee,* or *BIG.*

Citizen Dividends and *Citizen's Income* (in both, with or without *'s* or *s'* on *Citizen*) emphasize that this is for citizens, though some versions include legal residents. *Common heritage dividend* honors Thomas Paine's idea that land is "the common heritage of mankind." *Social Security for All* echoes Robert Theobald's suggestion that "Basic Economic Security can be best regarded as an extension of the present Social Security system."

Other names include *Dividends for All, National Tax Rebate, State Bonus, State Grants, Universal Allocation, Universal Benefit,* and *Universal Refundable Credit Income Tax.* New terms are likely to emerge in various countries and for local campaigns.

3. Chapter 3, page 31. The quote and the 6.1 billion hour figure are from a New York Times story in January, 2013. http://www.nytimes.com/2013/01/09/business/irss-taxpayer-advocate-calls-for-a-tax-code-overhaul.html.

4. Chapter 3, page 36. One group calling for Universal Child Benefits is the Niskanen Center, a self-described libertarian think tank. Their plan is "$2,000 per child under the age of 18, phased out for high income households," and they describe it as "a guaranteed minimum income for kids." They estimate that it "could be paid for several times over by consolidating some existing child programs and streamlining the complex and fragmented bureaucracy." https://niskanencenter.org/wp-content/uploads/2016/10/Universal ChildBenefit_final.pdf.

5. Chapter 3, page 36. "Class warfare," normally, is mere rhetoric, typically an attack or counterattack. In this instance, however, we can cite a widely-respected authority: billionaire investor Warren Buffett. "There's class warfare, all right, but It's my class,

the rich class, that's making the war, and we're winning." His tax rate is much lower than his secretary pays. http://www.nytimes. com/2006/11/26/business/yourmoney/26every.html.

6. Chapter 4, page 47. The EITC only helps low-wage workers, nothing for the unemployed. It requires people to file extra tax forms; many poor workers miss out because they fail to file or make mistakes. And it renders low-wage workers more afraid of losing their jobs, therefore afraid to ask for sick leave, higher pay, better hours, parental leave, or a union. Consequently, perhaps deliberately, the EITC indirectly subsidizes companies that pay the lowest wages — covert corporate welfare for Walmart and McDonald's.

7. Chapter 5, page 61. These criticisms of GDP are common. "The Trouble with GDP," from *The Economist* on April 30, 2016, presents the criticisms and the reasons to consider alternatives. http://www.economist.com/news/briefing/21697845-gross-domestic-product-gdp-increasingly-poor-measure-prosperity-it-not-even.

Economist Herman Daly and theologian John B. Cobb discuss GDP and alternative indicators in *For the Common Good: Redirecting the Economy toward Community, the Environment, and a Sustainable Future* (1989, and a 1994 second edition, co-written with). Economic welfare peaked in the mid 1970s, according to their analyses. Since then, most "growth" has been in activities that harm our society and our environment. Daly extends and elaborates on these themes in *Beyond Growth: The Economics of Sustainable Development* (1996).

8. Chapter 7, page 82. Voting is important though overemphasized, while other factors are often overlooked. Voting does not define democracy. An alternative is sortition, selecting officials at random

for a limited time, like a grand jury. Ideally, officials are anonymous, serve limited terms, and act in groups to provide diversity. Officials have compelling reasons to be reflective and responsible: their term ends, and then they have to live under the laws and policies they conceived.

The world's first democracy, ancient Athens, used sortition. They viewed it as superior to elections, possibly essential for a true democracy, because all citizens were clearly equal. With elections, Athenians found, wealthy oligarchs could buy their way into office. We've seen that. Perhaps we should use sortition.

9. Chapter 7, page 84. A history of corporate personhood is *Unequal Protection: the Rise of Corporate Dominance and the Theft of Human Rights* (2002) by author, entrepreneur, and television host Thom Hartmann.

Corporations Are Not People: Why They Have More Rights Than You Do and What You Can Do About It (2012), by lawyer and activist Jeffrey D. Clements, focuses on the *Citizens United* decision in 2010 — and the reasons we must overturn it.

10. Chapter 8, page 91. Before the 1990s, environmental concerns were nonpartisan.

Republican President Richard Nixon signed the Clean Air Act, Clean Water Act, Endangered Species Act, and the law that established the Environmental Protection Agency. Republican President Ronald Reagan was a leader in negotiating and implementing the Montreal Protocol, a strict international agreement to phase out ozone-depleting chemicals. Republican President George H. W. Bush declared himself the "environmental president," updated the Clean Air Act, and enacted a cap-and-trade program that reduced the sulfur dioxide emissions that cause acid rain.

The partisan split began while Democrat Bill Clinton was president. Special interests were and are the driving force, primarily the fossil fuel industry. Over the past two decades, increasingly, Republican politicians have proclaimed their eagerness to dig coal, drill for oil, issue permits, and rescind regulations.

11. Chapter 8, page 97. The benefits of land value taxes are most evident in Japan, Taiwan, and Hong Kong. Japan and Taiwan were poor countries prior to World War II. After the war, both instituted land value taxation (for different reasons), and the decline in land speculation helped transform both into economic powers. In Hong Kong, the land is owned by the public. Privately-owned buildings pay a ground rent. When the government invests in schools, police, mass transit, etc., land values go up; the gains are taxed and returned to the community.

In the United States, many places have a "split-rate" property tax that mainly taxes land values, with a lower rate on building values. Although this is not a full land value tax "experience in Pennsylvania and Maryland has shown that … [it] lowers property taxes on homeowners and vastly increases new construction and infill construction in urban areas," according to R. Joshua Vincent at the Center for the Study of Economics in Philadelphia. Their website is www.urbantoolsconsult.org.

Another useful resource is *Land Value Taxation: Theory, Evidence, and Practice* (2009). The editors are Richard F. Dye and Richard W. England, associates of the Lincoln Institute of Land Policy in Cambridge, MA.

12. Chapter 8, page 100. E. G. Vallianotos was a program analyst at the Environmental Protection Agency for 25 years, mostly in the Office of Pesticides Programs. In *Poison Spring: the Secret*

232 BASIC INCOME IMPERATIVE

History of Pollution and the EPA (2014), he and co-author McKay Jenkins (a professor of English, Journalism, and Environmental Humanities at the University of Delaware) document how the EPA was captured by the chemical, petroleum, and agribusiness industries. The EPA, they say, mainly functions as a "polluters' protection agency."

13. Chapter 8, page 102. Information about GMOs and glyphosate is from *Poison Spring*.

14. Chapter 8, page 102. A peer-reviewed scientific paper on Corexit and the Deepwater Horizon disaster, http://journals.plos. org/plosone/article?id=10.1371/journal.pone.0045574.

An article about the science and the politics, from Mother Jones magazine, http://www.motherjones.com/environment/2010/09/bp-ocean-dispersant-corexit.

15. Chapter 8, page 102. Plastic trash in the oceans has been widely reported. A National Geographic article from January 2015, http://news.nationalgeographic.com/news/2015/01/150109-oceans-plastic-sea-trash-science-marine-debris/.

Chapter 9, page 112. Worldwide weapon sales in 2015 totaled $80 billion. Half was from the United States; France was second at only $15 billion. The major buyers were Qatar, Egypt, Saudi Arabia, South Korea, and Pakistan. http://www.nytimes.com/2016/12/26/us/politics/united-states-global-weapons-sales.html.

16. Chapter 10, page 124. Democrats and Republicans are equally guilty of gerrymandering, and often collude to protect their respective districts. A few states, including Arizona and California, have

nonpartisan redistricting, though in each case enacting it required years of struggle.

17. Chapter 10, page 124. Nearly all politicians say they support full disclosure. It won't happen until We the People force them to act.

18. Chapter 10, page 124. Seattle is implementing a voucher program, approved by both the city council and a voter referendum in 2015. Every voter will get four $25 vouchers in each two-year election cycle.

http://www.nytimes.com/2015/11/08/opinion/sunday/in-seattle-a-campaign-finance-plan-that-voters-control.html.

Lawyer and professor of law Richard Hasen calls for vouchers in *Plutocrats United: Campaign Money, the Supreme Court, and the Distortion of American Elections* (2016).

Former Bush administration chief ethics officer Richard W. Painter proposes a federal tax rebate of $200 that taxpayers would allocate to selected political campaigns. He's now co-chair of Citizens for Responsibility and Ethics in Washington. His book is *Taxation Only With Representation: The Conservative Conscience and Campaign Finance Reform* (2016).

19. Chapter 10, page 125. Maine voters passed a ballot initiative in 2016 for Ranked Choice Voting (sometimes called Instant Runoff Voting, Preference Voting, or Alternative Voting).

From a month before the 2016 election, http://www.nytimes.com/2016/10/08/opinion/howard-dean-how-to-move-beyond-the-two-party-system.html.

And the morning after, http://www.slate.com/articles/business/moneybox/2016/11/maine_just_passed_ranked_choice_voting_bravo.html.

20. Chapter 10, page 125. In California's 2016 primaries for U.S. Senate and many other offices, the top two were Democrats. Democrats hold all statewide offices, with a supermajority in both houses of the state legislature. Top-four with RCV will be far more democratic.

21. Chapter 10, page 125. Reforming the Federal Election Commission may be imperative for restoring trust in our electoral system. Voter turnout in 2016 was only 55 percent. In years with no presidential election, turnout is normally below 50 percent, sometimes 30 percent or less.

Roughly 40 percent of Americans claim to be independent or unaffiliated. A seven-member FEC – two Democrats, two Republicans, and three who are neither – would provide meaningful checks and balances. Voter turnout is likely to increase, perhaps significantly.

We might create a Nonpartisan Commission to vet and nominate independent members.

This approach, adding nonpartisan members, could also be helpful with other government agencies, federal, state, and local.

22. Chapter 10, page 125. This is only a partial list. It leaves off term limits, for example, and proposals to make political campaigns shorter and more sensible. Many of the listed reforms are already being considered in a few states or nationally.

For more information about the National Popular Vote and proportional representation with multi-member districts, a good source is FairVote, a nonpartisan group that's been working on these issues since 1992. www.fairvote.org. (They've also been leaders on RCV.)

23. Chapter 10, page 128. These figures are from a March 2017 article about the size, cost, reach, and power of the U.S. military. https://www.nytimes.com/interactive/2017/03/22/us/is-americas-military-big-enough.html.

24. Chapter 10, page 131. Of the two that were not ratified, one is now the Twenty-Seventh Amendment, added in 1992. "No law, varying the compensation for the services of the Senators and Representatives, shall take effect, until an election of representatives shall have intervened."

25. Chapter 10, page 134. The rebels in Boston were demanding true self-government. If modern Tea Party activists fully embrace their namesakes' ideals and goals, including sovereignty over corporations, Americans are likely to benefit for many generations.

26. Chapter 10, page 134. Activists from the left and the right are organizing to overturn *Citizens United*. That may be impossible unless we resolve core issues with corporate personhood. Two helpful books are in note #9.

27. Chapter 11, page 138. "Inverted" is from Sheldon Wolin, who was a professor emeritus of politics at Princeton University. In *Democracy Incorporated: Managed Democracy and the Specter of Inverted Totalitarianism* (2008), he analyzed economic power and how it dominates our politics. Today, as he described, private corporations are both the agents of our government and its masters, managing it – and us – to serve their interests. Corporations rule. Nearly everyone complies with their requests and demands, and most of us comply without asking any questions. America is becoming, or already is, a new type of totalitarian state.

Democracy, he wrote, is "about the conditions that make it possible for ordinary people to better their lives by becoming political beings and by making power responsive to their hopes and needs." We the People have to assert our sovereignty over corporations. Our government must be truly ours: real people only.

28. Chapter 12, page 149. When people call for pilot projects, they typically express concerns about folks quitting jobs and squandering the money. That hasn't happened. Appendices 1 and 3 review numerous pilots and experiments: none has revealed widespread problems. Research clearly shows that people make good decisions and use the money responsibly.

Acknowledgments

The core of this book, for me, is the way of thinking that led to these ideas and the reader-centered presentation. I especially thank two mentors, though both are no longer alive. Moshe Feldenkrais was an engineer, mathematician, neuroscientist, judo master, and the creator of the Feldenkrais Method of somatic education. I view him primarily as a philosopher. Thinking, he avowed, is more fundamental than language; words often thwart, distort, or distract us from thinking; and "real thinking leads to new ways of acting." He acted to "make the abstract concrete." He aspired to "say yes and no at the same time."

Robert Fitzgerald was a "recovering attorney," devoted environmentalist, and steadfast advocate for system science and rigorous thinking. Bob insisted on refining or distilling ideas first, before considering any presentation, and I practice that when I write anything. I especially thank him for "There is no *we*," which he routinely whispered at meetings and lectures. When I wrote my first book about basic income, he was my first reader, and his suggestions were invariably valuable. While writing this book, I often wished he was available.

Moshe and Bob were true mentors, as distinct from teachers. They encouraged me to trust my insights, guided me to question abstract concepts, and challenged me to think concretely and functionally. Their influence is everywhere throughout this book.

Another significant influence was the book *Disclosing New Worlds*, by Charles Spinosa, Fernando Flores, and Hubert L. Dreyfus. I was also inspired by, and applied, two methods for making decisions. ORID (Objective, Reflective, Interpretive, Decisional) is a group facilitation process, developed by the Institute of Cultural Affairs. I thank J.W. Ballard and Don Cramer for educating me. OODA (Observe, Orient, Decide, Act) loop is from Col. John Boyd, a preeminent military strategist. Thanks to Bill Moyer for introducing me to Chuck Spinney, and to Chuck for a briefing on Boyd and "Motherhood and Mismatch."

I've talked about the ideas in this book with thousands of people over several decades, and I'd like to thank everyone. Through your listening and your questions – even if you doubted, objected, or bluntly rejected what I was saying – I learned to refine my ideas and my skills in communicating. You helped me and I thank you.

Extra thanks to everyone in the basic income community. If you attended any meeting of USBIG, BIEN, or Basic Income Action, even if we never spoke, you boosted my commitment and confidence. Specifically, in roughly chronological order of our first contact, thanks to Jeffrey J. Smith, Gary Flomenhoft, Mike Livingston, Alanna Hartzok, Al Sheahen, Karl Widerquist, Eri Noguchi, Michael Lewis, Almaz Zelleke, Guy Standing, Philippe van Parijs, Eduardo Matarazzo Suplicy, Michael Howard, Sean Healy, Bridget Reynolds, Jason Murphy, Ingrid van Neikerk, and Scott Santens. Thanks also to Diane Pagen, Dan O'Sullivan, Ian Schlakman, Mark Witham, and Tristan Roberts. And to Kate McFarland.

I began writing in early 2011, completed the manuscript in late 2015, and revised it throughout the 2016 election. I'd like to thank Donald Trump, Hillary Clinton, Bernie Sanders, Ted Cruz, Jill Stein,

Gary Johnson, and other candidates – along with a wide range of pundits, journalists, and activists – for providing countless opportunities to test my ideas and refine my presentation.

For help with my initial efforts to find a publisher, sincere thanks to Ralph Nader, Phil Spitzer, and Lucas Ortiz. Ironic thanks to the many agents, editors, and publishers who passed on my queries and proposals.

Special thanks to my excellent, professional, anonymous editor. You improved the manuscript immensely, and helped me become a better writer. I hope you like the changes I made after your edits and suggestions. (She works for diverse politicians and other public figures, and insists on anonymity with nonfiction projects.)

I compiled the material in Appendix 1 over three decades, and have published several prior iterations. This version is the most comprehensive by far, with a number of items I learned about rather recently, thanks to Allen Sheahen, Philippe Van Parijs, Guy Standing, and Karl Widerquist. Thanks to Rick Rybeck, Alanna Hartzok, and Dave Wetzel for responding to questions about the land value tax. Thanks to Rob Ritchie and Cynthia Terrell at Fairvote.

I've had a good experience with BookBaby, and I thank everyone I've interacted with. I may use them again.

Family and friends have supported me emotionally and financially. Thanks to my mother above all, and to my father, brothers, and sister. Also thanks to George Ripley, John Clausen, Lone Hansen, Heidi Thompson, and "Tuesdays at Two." I also thank my FlexAware students for tolerating my absences.

Enthusiastic thanks, in advance, to everyone who helps enact these ideas. If you decide to run for political office, I'll do what I can to assist with your campaign. Let's make history.